GK

BIZARRE BUILDINGS

BIZARRE
BUILDINGS

Paul Cattermole
with Ian Westwell

COMPENDIUM

COMPENDIUM

Published by 2007 by Compendium Publishing Limited, 1st Floor, 43 Frith Street, London W1D 4SA

ISBN 978-1-905573-71-4

Designed by Cara Rogers

Printed in China through Printworks In't. Ltd.

Acknowledgments

Thanks to Sandra Forty for extra text and captions. Photo research was by Paul Cattermole and Sandra Forty: thanks to Ruth Marler at Arcaid, Katie Johnston at Corbis, Marc Seigerman at Getty Images and Gwyn Headley at fotoLibra. Individual photograph credits are as follows:

arcaid.co.uk
2–3, 5, 60–61, 130–131, 152, 154–155, Architekturphoto; 156, 157, 158–159, Ralph Richter/Architekturphoto; 5, 13R, 54, 55, 90–91, 99, 100, 108, 110, 113–115, 122, 123, 168, 169, 183, 184, 190–193, 197, 204, 212–213, Richard Bryant; 5, 119, 162–163, Benedict Luxmoore; 9, Richard Waite; 11, 120, 153, 188, 189, John Edward Linden; 12, 48, 49, Michael Harding; 13L, David Soulsby; 18, 76, 185T, 186–187, Alex Bartel; 50, 51, 52, Richard Powers; 56, 57, 74, 75, 77–84, 86–89, Alan Weintraub; 59, 132, 133, 215, Marcel Malherbe; 66, 67, Jonathan Miller; 73, Lucinda Lambton; 98, Joe Cornish; 101, 103–105, 138, 182, Bill Tingey; 102, Peter Aaron/Esto; 116T, 118, 139–141, 143, 146, 170–175, Nick Kane; 134–135, 137, Floto + Warner; 148, 149, Natalie Tepper; 160, 161,

Mark Fiennes; 166, 167, I.B. Aguirre; 180, 181, Kadu Niemeyer; 185B, Richard Einzig; 194, 195, Renzo Piano; 214, Farrel Grehan.

Corbis
1, Paul Miller/epa; 20, 21, 23T, Forestier Patrick/Corbis Sygm 23B, Corbis Sygma; 38, Herbert Spichtinger/zefa/Corbis; 39, Gregor M. Schmid; 44, 45L, 45R, Harald Jahn; 46–47 , Franz–Marc Frei; 62L, Gregor Schuster/zefa/Corbis; 62R, 63, Archivo Iconografico, S.A.; 64, David Samuel Robbins; 65, Peter Aprahamian; 68, Jeffrey L. Rotman; 198T, Eberhard Streichan/zefa/Corbis; 198B, Yann Arthus–Bertrand; 199 (both), Txema Fernandez/epa; 200, 201 Jose Fuste Raga.

fotoLibra
5, 10, 14L, 16–17, 29, 164, 216, Sue Walker; 5, 42–43, 58, Tina Bout; 14R, 165, Matthew Dearsley; 15, Andy Myatt; 19, Howard Mellowes; 24, 25L, Gill Jones; 25R, 106, 121, Gwyn Headley; 26, 28, Karen Kelly; 27, Dave Symington; 30T, Kim Comber; 30B, 31, 125, Tigran Asatrajan; 32, 33, Rudi Tapper; 34, Colin Dixon; 35, Farhood Azar II; 36L, Huw Alban; 36R, David Young; 37, Geoff Gartside; 53, KRiZ CPEc; 69, 70–71, Rob Langhorst; 72, John Riley; 85, 217R, Robert Down; 92, Jennifer Green; 93, Peter Vallance; 94, Andy Whitehead; 95, 96, 97, 112, 129, Keith Erskine; 109, Dominic Arkwright; 111, Richard Gillespie; 116B, T.G. Riches; 117, Gil Gillis; 124, Sarah Isaacs; 126, 127, 136, Patrick Tweddle; 128, Peter Bassett; 142, Ricardo Pimentel; 144–145, 150, Jenny Brice; 147, Raymond Lofthouse; 151, Arnold de Bruin; 176, 177 Bryan Smith; 196, David Knowles; 202, Al Sermeno; 203, Ian Walker; 205, John Short; 206–207, Paul Hurst; 208, Guy Sargent; 209, John Gilkerson; 210–211, Martin Hendry; 217L Graham Herbert; 218, John Launay; 219, Peter Herbert; 220, 221, Jan Traylen; 223, Gail Johnson.

Getty Images
22, Science Faction; 40–41, Doug Armand/Stone; 107, Aurora; 178, AFP; 179, Bongarts.

Cover photos:
Front: Getty-Science Faction
Back: TL—Tina Bout/fotoLibra; CL—Gil Gillis/fotoLibra; BL—Alan Weintraub/arcaid.co.uk; TR—Gwyn Headley/fotoLibra; BR—Aurora/Getty Images

CONTENTS

FOREWORD

Is there any reason why New Zealand's Parliament Building in Wellington should resemble a futuristic tanklike robot emerging from the pavement?

Mankind came down from the trees, sheltered in caves and then ventured into the construction industry. One of the earliest names to be preserved through history is Imhotep, architect to Egypt's pharaohs, who lived nearly 4,700 years ago. He built the Step Pyramid, which still stands at Saqqara, and became a god, a transition not unwelcome to many present-day architects.

The proper collective noun for them is An Arrogance of Architects, but the buildings arrayed here exude a sense of humor, confidence, despair, vanity, incompetence, glory, nervousness, braggadocio and madness far in excess of what is normally expected from the generally agreeable members of that ancient and honorable profession. That's because often the shape and form of many of these architectural eccentricities has been dictated by the patron or client. Cutting-edge design can veer toward the knife edge of insanity because it's difficult to approach this most serious of arts in a lighthearted manner. Like the bar room bore with just one joke, humor in stone doesn't go away and can quickly pall. Amusement is literally petrified.

A few open-minded businessmen (almost never women) unencumbered by a band of ascetic shareholders manage to create confections of wonder, like the United Equipment Company in California, but mere individuals can no longer compete with the astonishing budgets lavished on pet projects by politicians and museum directors. In some cases the vision bears real and lasting fruit: Bilbao, a grim, violent, industrial town in the Basque Country of northern Spain, became an improbable tourist destination after the opening of Frank Gehry's iconic and bizarre Guggenheim museum.

The first function of buildings was to provide shelter and a place to gather. That remains an important consideration today. Then came monumental architecture, the pyramid formalizing a pile of stones. Two thousand years ago we had progressed sufficiently to be able to construct circular and oval buildings out of brick and stone. All the while the basic tools were the rule, plumb line and square; a building's primary purpose has always been to stay standing up. It was always cheaper and easier to build in straight lines. There may be more interior space in an egg than a cube, but it's a lot harder to use. So around the world the simplest buildings grew to the same basic formula: four walls and a roof, pitched so the rain could run off. And that's what every child will draw. Only when excess money was added to the equation could the rules be curved.

The creation of the great Gothic cathedrals of Europe, oratorios in stone, was credited to master masons who carried out the role and function of architects. Stone masons were masters of their material, cognizant of the density, stress and load-bearing abilities of masonry as different as friable sandstone and solid granite. Science had not yet discovered metals that could compete. All that was to change in the 18th century.

Ironbridge is a small town in Shropshire, England. It is so named because it grew up around a bridge built of iron. Before this, all permanent bridges had been constructed of wood or stone, but as the furnaces in Coalbrookdale were producing tons of iron, Abraham Darby III—an ironmaster rather than an architect—thought he would try his hand at bridging the River Severn with this cheap, malleable material. So here in 1779 he built the first iron bridge. Ever. This defines disruptive technology. Now every new bridge in the world owes more to Darby's graceful revolution than to the preceding two millennia.

Technology spreads unevenly. The Myceneans couldn't conceive the arch. They tried to create it by propping two stones together. The Egyptians and the Arabs couldn't figure out how to support a large roof span other than with a forest of columns: entering the Temple at Karnak and the Grand Mosque at Cordoba is like walking through a stone grove. But eventually we all learned how to do stuff, and ambition became limited only by the properties of the materials used. The necessity for the rectangle had gone. New Zealanders can now foregather in a robot simply because they can. They have the technology.

It takes much to surprise us today. Fifty years ago any deviation from a rectilinear norm would have the natives spluttering into their beers and concocting improbable stories on the inevitable fate of the occupants. And fit for purpose was ensuring that a house had, at the least, two up two down, with a front and back door, and wasn't shaped like a shoe (United States) or a horse (Greece).

So many people live in converted churches that it has now become commonplace. But to clad three workers' cottages with lancet windows and place a high sham tower at the end so they resembled a village church became a source of wonder for 200 years in the east of England.

Look at The Pineapple in Scotland. Yes, it's a stone fruit, 50 times life size, but the architect remains anonymous. Whoever he was, he did a superb job because each individual leaf is curved and drained to allow water to run off and prevent the formation of ice — which would snap off the leaf — and despite long periods of neglect it looks as immaculate and amazing today as it did when it was built 250 years ago.

Mud, wood, stone, iron, glass, steel, carbon-fiber, titanium and yet more exotic metals chart the progression of material technology in building. Today's architectural flights of fancy are no longer assembled by the unemployed being paid a wage to win a squire's wager. They are hi-tech constructions of carbon-fiber and titanium, soaring over spaces in a way that humbler materials, such as brick, mortar and lime, could only dream of doing.

New technology means new and fanciful forms can be conceived. The role of the architect, primarily to clothe space, is now yielding to the competence of the structural engineer. The architect still has the vision of what he wants to achieve, but now the engineer is playing an increasingly important — but less feted — role. The architect dreams, the engineer creates. But the downside of taking the credit means that when the building collapses — as buildings still do — it's the architect who gets the publicity, before the structural engineer.

Nothing captures the zeitgeist more accurately than architecture. A little learning is all it takes — no great study is needed to be able to walk down most city streets in the world and pinpoint the buildings to the nearest decade. Every generation brings forth two or three pioneers, working at the pointed edge of the profession, admired and aped by students who graduate and produce weak oblations to the new vocabulary. Compromised by clients and constrained by budgets, the followers do the best they can with their limited vision, and a new city grows with easily datable buildings for later generations to smile at in recognition.

Now every museum worth its admission charge has to have a wibbly-wobbly roof (a technical term that may previously have eluded you) or be clad in undulating sheets of some rare and opulent metallic element. The few exceptions to this new order directive are sports stadiums, the cathedrals of the third millennium. Here architectural eccentricity is eschewed in favor of packing down as many seats as health and safety authorities will permit. The Romans wrote the book with the Colosseum, and 2,000 years of progress have barely changed the basic concept.

The Selfridges building in Birmingham is the antithesis of the old Sullivan dictate that form follows function. It's that shape because it can be, not because its use demanded it. And just in case you suspect I hold a Panglossian view of unusual architecture, I think it's a hideous eyesore and deserves to be torn down immediately.

The most vulnerable decade for a building is when it's 30 to 40 years old. The architecture will be unspeakably ugly, the structure will be impractical and expensive to maintain. It will look shoddy and unloved. The architect himself will be unfashionable and probably harbor inappropriate political views. Any move to tear it down will quickly gain popular support.

In the past many unnecessarily extravagant buildings were dismissed as follies. But very few buildings are inexplicably mad; in the main a folly is a misunderstood building. The word folly came from foolishness or madness, so the term was applied derogatorily to a building the viewer didn't understand. But an interesting alternative is that the word originated from the French *feuillée* — leafy — often applied to a copse of the top of a hill. England has many hills crowned with a ring of trees with no indication that a building stood anywhere nearby, yet the hill is often called The Folly. The meaning of the word changes.

All words endure shifts in meaning. The word bizarre has come down to us through various disputed origins, including the Basque word for beard, to mean "brave" and "handsome," before slouching into the demimonde of the odd and peculiar.

This fantastic collection of buildings around the world must reinstate those earlier interpretations of the word. These monstrous erections can all be described as bold and daring, innovative adventures in architecture. Some are handsome, some are merely good-looking and some could only be loved by their mother.

Bizarre? Or brave, handsome buildings? Look through this impressive selection and dare to decide.

Gwyn Headley
Founder, The Folly Fellowship

INTRODUCTION
THE ODD, THE ECCENTRIC & THE EXTRAVAGANT

bizarre / bi'zah/ **adj 1** odd, eccentric or extravagant. **2** involving sensational contrasts or incongruities

The New Penguin English Dictionary

This is a book of outrageous oddities and extravagant exceptions, of buildings that brazenly invite the prefix of "bizarre." But for these sensational structures to be considered "exceptions to the rule" there must be rules to begin with. Few creative disciplines are fonder of formulating rules than architecture, that aristocrat of the applied arts, whose practitioners have spent centuries literally drawing up the fabric of our urban world. These rules come in many forms, permeating every level of the profession, from the mundane building regulations to the highbrow minefield that is the "ism." Constructivism, brutalism, expressionism, postmodernism — the proliferation of schools of architectural thought throughout the 20th century has left a rich legacy of buildings, but without always leaving the layman with any easy explanation as to their underlying rationale. This is modern architecture's Achilles' heel, the veil of elitism that can so easily prevent those outside of the profession from being able to relate to the buildings that surround them. Great architecture has the power to excite and engage all who come into contact with it, inviting the viewer to offer his or her own interpretation and judgment. The stories behind a building, the hidden narratives of architecture, need to be shared.

This is not intended as a scholarly survey into every intricacy of architectural thought but as a visual primer, an accessible introduction to the wild side of a discipline that has the power to change the way we live but can all too often be content to follow a path well-trod. This is a collection of projects that dared to be different, instead of follow the herd. They are not drawn together by a unified movement, a convenient "ism" with which to be pigeonholed. They are themselves. Put simply, they are "bizarre buildings."

ODD ARCHITECTURE — TIME AND PLACE

To modern eyes many of the architectural styles of bygone eras appear fanciful, far-fetched and, frankly, bizarre. The whiplash tendrils of art nouveau, the voluptuous excesses of the rococo and baroque, the soaring spires and forests of flying buttresses of the Gothic. All appear a world away to 21st-century city dwellers, conditioned by years spent in a largely rectilinear environment, a "bungaloid dystopia," as the satirical writer Julian Barnes once dubbed the spreading sea of suburban clones in *England, England* (Random House, 1998).

Architecture is just as susceptible to trends and fads as clothes and music, the astute architect often being able to adapt his style to keep in sync with his potential clients' aspirations. Yet, occasionally, you find a building so unique that is out of step, not only with the conventions of its own time but also seemingly with reality itself. One particularly fine example is the Pineapple House in Dunmore, Stirlingshire, a textbook example of "the folly." The great architectural critic Sir Nikolaus Pevsner defined the folly in *The Penguin Dictionary of Architecture* (Fourth Edition, Penguin Books, 1991) as "a costly but useless structure built to satisfy the whim of some eccentric and thought to show his folly," but whereas most take the form of picturesque ruins, ancient Greek temples or fairy-tale mock-medieval towers, the Pineapple House chooses to emulate an exotic piece of flora, native to a distant shore. The background to its construction is worthy of consideration as it presents the concept of architecture as narrative, as a record of customs, traditions and personalities, a recurring theme throughout the projects in this book.

In 1761 John Murray, the 4th Earl of Dunmore, chose to construct a typically Georgian Palladian garden pavilion in the grounds of his estate, containing a hothouse, where tropical plants could be cultivated, sheltered from the cold, inclement Scottish climate. The two stone urns that stand at either side of the portico are in fact disguised chimneys for the fires that kept the delicate specimens at a temperature to which they were accustomed — a neat sleight of hand that prevented the classical exterior from being marred by anything as unromantic as an industrial flue. Having created his hothouse, the earl left his home to serve as the governor of the colonies of New York and Virginia and did not return from his duties until 1777. Some time after this date he chose to make an unorthodox addition to his previous structure: a summer house in the shape of a 37 foot (11 meter) high stone pineapple. The basic form is a hexagonal cupola over a banqueting room, with delicate pointed Gothic windows, whose peaked frames blend seamlessly into the lower leaves of the organic dome. The workmanship is of the finest quality, with each leaf being individually carved and shaped to allow rainwater to drain away, preventing frost damage.

But why would a Scottish earl choose to lavish such expense on an inedible masonry fruit? The simple truth is that no concrete evidence exists for the motives or justification for such a structure, or even the identity of its architect. Several names have been put forward, including that of William Chambers, designer of Somerset House and of many buildings in Kew Gardens, but there are no papers to corroborate this. What is known, however, is that a quaint tradition existed among the wealthy gentlemen who owned both grand houses in the eastern American colonies and plantations in the West Indies. There the pineapple was regarded as a symbol of welcome, and these gentlemen, returning from trips to survey their plantations, would place a real pineapple on their gatepost as a sign that they were once more in residence and ready to receive guests.

It does not seem far-fetched to imagine the returning governor of the colonies translating this quaint folk tradition from across the Atlantic into a novel piece of garden architecture, which would make the Pineapple House the product of a wry Scottish wit rather than a straightforward act of eccentric folly.

BELOW Like a flamboyant table centrepiece for a regal Georgian banquet, the ornate Pineapple House's dome forms a tropical crown to an aristocratic Palladian hothouse.

ECCENTRIC ARCHITECTURE — DIVINE ENGINEERING

The Pineapple House is a modest affair compared with the monumental works of Spain's most flamboyant and original architect, Antoni Gaudi. His work, too, is characterized by a high level of craftsmanship, combined with a mind-boggling depth of detailing that helped to define a style that was all his own. A church, a reverential house of God, may seem an odd structure to include in a book of "bizarre buildings," but few who have seen the tapered towers of the Sagrada Familia would claim them to be an essay in conventional ecclesiastical architecture. This project came to dominate Gaudi's life from the time he took over the works from the original architect, Francisco del Villar, in 1883 until his fatal collision with a tram in 1926. From 1914 he worked on no other project, devoting himself entirely to the monument that was to become his greatest legacy in Barcelona. Little of the structure we see today was completed in Gaudi's own lifetime. Only the tower of St Barnabas reached its full height before the architect met his end. It forms one of a quartet of spires that dominate the Nativity facade, the most photographed elevation of the building and one that appears on countless T-shirts, postcards and souvenirs, effectively becoming visual shorthand for the whole city.

At first glance these conical pinnacles, emblazoned with text and embellished with mosaic finials, seem purely sculptural, a very organic interpretation of the traditional European cathedral Gothic. Yet these elongated spires are essentially a work of modern engineering, a group of mutually supportive

columns that enables them to achieve heady heights from a narrow footprint. Gaudi's visual virtuosity was developed with the aid of sophisticated scale models, some of which were composed of successive webs of suspended strings and weights, held taught by gravity, then positioned over large mirrors so that their dangling reflections appeared to point to the sky. If you imagine the clusters of spires hanging down like ornate stalactites from the ceiling of some mythical cavern, it is easy to grasp how this design process came to affect the overall aesthetic and how gravity, a force of nature, was harnessed to calculate the loads and stresses.

The long, downward slanting slots that perforate the spires' sides are another hint to the science of Gaudi's art. Wrapped tightly inside the narrow towers are spiral staircases so steep that their overlapping outer edges form a natural handrail, omitting the need for a banister. The steps are cantilevered out from the inner walls, leaving the central "eye" of the towers to form a long, hollow chamber. Gaudi saw the Sagrada Familia as a way of reconnecting the people of Barcelona with their God and intended to broadcast his message across the city. This he did in the conventional manner of densely packed facades (so dripping with figurative sculpture and foliage that they resemble a folly's grotto), but also with clever acoustics. His plans included using the hollow towers to accommodate long tubular bells, hanging freely down their centers, with each tower housing a different pitch, transforming the facade into an immense organ capable of directing its sustained notes out into the streets. The slots also afford glimpses of people ascending the spiral stairs, bringing to mind Constantin Brancusi's definition of architecture as "inhabited sculpture," or of termites busily traversing their tapered mound. The slots lighten the structure, reducing the wind loads and ventilating the confines of the staircases, a useful bonus for the dedicated pilgrim sweating up the spiraling flights to gaze out over the city.

Gaudi's architecture was already out of favor when he died, and his style spent the next 60 years as a footnote, an eccentric stylistic cul-de-sac in the development of architecture. Indeed, it is only in the last quarter of the 20th century that his work was afforded a serious reevaluation by architectural critics, including Pevsner, and given the academic kudos to match his popular acclaim. Gaudi's work is now celebrated, not only in his native Catalonia but also the world over. His style may have been individual, but the integrity of his structures and the way he seamlessly integrated his engineering with his art arguably elevates them from the bizarre to the sublime.

EXTRAVAGANT ARCHITECTURE — INSTANT ICONS

Some 65 years after Gaudi's death, a lone man took a solitary morning jog along the banks of the Nervion River in the northern Spanish town of Bilbao. He paused momentarily to gaze over a partially derelict site, occupied by a few nondescript warehouses and edged by a road bridge and a railway line. It was an unremarkable urban landscape in a town suffering from the predictable effects of the downturn in its traditional industries of fishing and ship

LEFT AND RIGHT The enchanted grove of the Sagrada Familia's spires rises out of the lake at their feet, the distinctive elongated slots intended to send their bells' sonorous notes echoing out into the city.

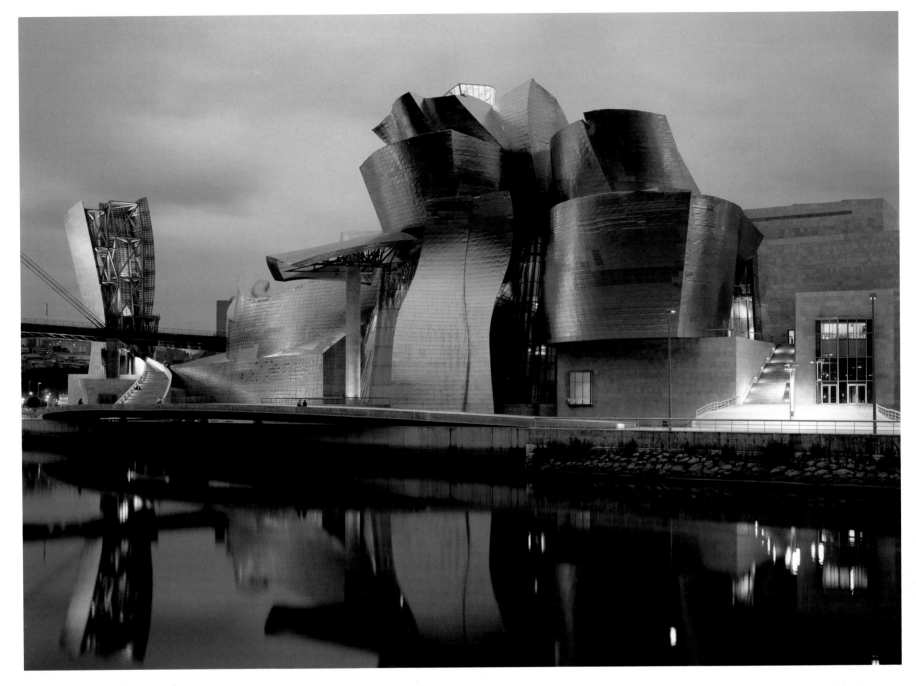

building. He resumed his morning perambulations but returned to his hotel room with a solution to the problem that had been vexing him: where to build the next Guggenheim museum. For that jogger was none other than Thomas Krens, director of the Solomon R. Guggenheim Foundation, an American institution, a colossus of the art world. He had been searching for a new European outpost where the foundation could display a portion of its collection, a collection so vast that only a fraction of it could be hung in Frank Lloyd Wright's famous spiraling gallery in New York. Krens appreciated that great art requires great architecture, and he put in motion a competition to select a design that would continue the foundation's legacy of enlightened architectural commissions. That competition was won by Frank Gehry, a Canadian-born

ABOVE, RIGHT AND FAR RIGHT Reflected in the waters of the Nervion, the Guggenheim Museum presents a jostling mass of sweeping titanium forms, like a fleet of deconstructed fishing boats riding a wave of culture.

architect based in California, and the museum he produced has gone down as one of the most remarkable and influential buildings of the 20th century.

Like Krens, Gehry saw the site as the perfect setting for a building that could respond to the city and form a gateway to the business and historic quarters. His design began as a series of rapid freehand sketches made on site and then taken back to his studio, where the energetic pen strokes were transformed into hundreds, if not thousands, of models. These were not staid scale models but masses of folded, twisted and crumpled paper and card, used to create apparently random forms that combined to become a building. Architects have always used models to test their ideas, but it was the way in which Gehry then translated his spontaneity directly into steel that marks the Guggenheim Bilbao as a quantum leap in building design. The physical models were spirited into the virtual world by scanning their irregular curves with a laser, the digital data then being exported into a computer program called CAITA. This was not a regular architectural tool but one borrowed from the aviation industry, where it had previously been used to design the Mirage jet fighter and the Boeing 777. Given this pedigree, the program had little difficulty adapting to Gehry's concept, one that amounted to an immense steel-framed fuselage, skinned in gleaming lock-seamed titanium plates. All the components were cut using computer numeric controlled (CNC) cutters guided by the data derived from the Gehry's model. As holes could be pre-drilled to an unparalleled degree of accuracy, the frame was bolted rather than welded together, the precut sections being brought to site to be assembled like a gigantic Meccano set. A projecting layer of curved-steel tubes was attached to the main skeleton, smoothing out its faceted edges into the graceful contours that support the shimmering skin we see today. The by-product of the architects, engineers and contractors all simultaneously sharing the same data was a project that was delivered on time and on budget, $86 (£44) million, without sacrificing any of the original model's sculptural panache along the way. It was as though Gehry had been able to mold the building with his own hands, which, in effect, he had.

SENSATIONAL CONTRASTS OR INCOHERENT INCONGRUITIES?

Gehry's innovative architectural approach produced one of the world's most instantly recognizable signature buildings and fueled an unprecedented rise in landmark projects, all intended to emulate the subsequent urban regeneration with which the museum is credited. Perhaps the project's highest accolade is that this phenomenon is now universally referred to as "the Bilbao effect." To quantify the Guggenheim's success one has only to look at how the number of visitors to Bilbao grew in the years following the grand opening. In 1998 there were 1.3 million more visitors than before the titanium hull came in to port, with 1.1 million in 1999, and a staggering 3 million the year after that. However, the concept of a single building transforming the fortunes of an entire city was not invented in Bilbao but more than three decades before and

half a world away in Australia. Back in 1973 Sydney's famous opera house proved that modern architecture had the power to attract tourists in by the thousands and put a previously sidelined city back on the world cultural map. It exceeded all expectations and remains Australia's most enduring manmade icon. In some respects, however, the much-vaunted opera house failed to meet its expectations. It has done little to extend the home audience for opera, exceeded the original budget several times over and took 16 highly fraught years to realize. By comparison, the immediacy of Gehry's miraculous five-year construction schedule magnified his building's impact and made the Guggenheim an instant icon. Tourists don't just walk around his museum, they go inside as well.

The quest for the "icon," the startling signature building with regenerative powers, is sweeping the cities of the world in what appears to be one gigantic architectural branding exercise. The critic Charles Jencks dryly observed in *The Iconic Building* (Frances Lincoln, 2005) that by the year 2000 architects and city governors from across the globe had absorbed the military ethos of "shock and awe" and adapted it to become "shock and tourism." The result was a swarm of increasingly bizarre buildings, all clamoring for column inches. If none have been quite as successful as the Guggenheim it is because there are simply too many buildings now vying for our attention. The constant game of one-upmanship has effectively created a state of architectural hyperinflation, the value and impact of each building being eclipsed by the next.

But there is another argument as to why the Guggenheim and Sydney Opera House have managed to sustain their success, despite a host of pretenders to their crowns. They are both what Jencks describes as "enigmatic signifiers," structures that are open to many interpretations, both subtle and obvious, but most crucially, almost always natural. The soaring concrete arches of the opera house can, and are, readily interpreted as billowing sails, scattered shells or breaking waves, whereas the Guggenheim invites comparisons with shoals of silvery fish, multiple ships' bows and the swirling waters of the Nervion. Their architects have picked their visual metaphors wisely, bedding their buildings into the local culture and landscape to give them genuine narrative qualities. Other buildings in this book have faired less favorably, with the public, their creators forgetting, in their haste to provide a sensational contrast to their peers, to tap into the context of the site. Instead of a big splash they make a loud "plop" and are ridiculed for being hopelessly incongruous, eyesores in all but name.

The chapters that follow offer up a survey of some of the world's most bizarre buildings, introducing the characters behind their conception, the supposed source of their aesthetics and the technology that makes them tick.

Are they jarring follies or charismatic enigmas? You decide.

Paul Cattermole

BELOW LEFT, BELOW AND RIGHT Sheltering in the shadows of their massive concrete shells, the Sydney Opera Houses' auditoriums escape the fierce heat of the Australian day. But when the sun sets, it is the opera houses' turn to shine, transforming itself into a beacon for the arts.

PAVILIONS & FOLLIES

GEODESIC DOME, MONTREAL, CANADA

The Montreal Biosphere is an interesting contradiction. Whereas true follies often take the form of functionless ruins, here Environment Canada has taken the burnt-out ruin of an engineering icon and reinvented it as a monument to the ecosystems of our planet. Designed by the prolific polymath, Richard Buckminster Fuller the Biosphere began life as the U.S. Pavilion for Montreal's Expo '67, showcasing the system of geodesics that Fuller patented in 1954. Using triangles and hexagons to divide up a sphere's surface, he created a self-supporting space frame, enclosing the maximum possible volume with the minimum surface area. Standing 200 feet (61 meters) tall and 250 feet (76 meters) wide, it was originally skinned in acrylic panels equipped with photovoltaic cells, but these were destroyed by fire in 1976, leaving the skeletal steel structure open to the elements. Erecting a new museum to the environment within its envelope was a suitably sustainable solution for recycling a building system that Fuller purposefully designed to be reused.

LE PALAIS IDÉAL, CHÂTEAUNEUF-DE-GALAURE, FRANCE

This bizarre building is the work of a French postman, Ferdinand Cheval (1836–August 19, 1924). Le Palais Idéal was started in April 1879: Cheval said that he tripped on a stone and was inspired by its shape. During his daily mail route and in retirement, Cheval carried stones at first in his pockets, then a basket and eventually a wheelbarrow. His self-inflicted task took him the next 33 years — there is an inscription on Le Palais Idéal that identifies "10,000 days, 9,300 hours, 33 years of toil." Cheval spent the first two decades building the outer walls — 85 feet (26 meters) long, 45 feet (14 meters) wide and up to 33 feet (10 meters) high — continuing after his retirement in 1896. He often worked at night in the light of an oil lamp. Locals regarded him as a village idiot, but before his death he began to receive some recognition from luminaries such as Pablo Picasso. The building is covered with inscriptions of all sorts, figures of many animals and famous people. In 1969 André Malraux, French minister of culture, declared the site a cultural landmark and had it officially protected.

Inside and outside Le Palais Idéal with (**BOTTOM**) a photograph of postman Ferdinand Cheval hard at work.

THE SACRED GROVE, BOMARZO, ITALY

RIGHT Bomarzo, near Rome in central Italy, is home to an extraordinary collection of sculptures on a forested hillside just below the small town. They were created by Duke Pierfrancesco Orsini, a soldier and diplomat who began planning his Sacred Grove in the late 1550s after a period of imprisonment and the death of his wife. The various sculptures, which were carved out of the natural volcanic rock under the guidance of Neopolitan architect Pirro Legario, are invariably monumental and often terrifying. The park was known to the frightened locals as the "Grove of Monsters" but was largely forgotten by the wider world until restoration work began in the 1950s.

OWL HOUSE, NIEU BETHESDA, SOUTH AFRICA

LEFT AND BELOW This much-transformed house and the sculptures of the associated Camel Yard can be found in the isolated village of Nieu Bethesda, South Africa, and were the singular vision of a reclusive former teacher, Helen Martins. "Miss Helen" embarked on the project in 1945, following the death of her parents. She initially worked on the house's drab interior, plastering the walls and ceilings with patterns of crushed glass in blocks of bright paint. She began the exterior sculpture park in the 1960s, largely aided by a local workman, Koos Madgas, who used cement and glass to create artworks inspired by Martins' fascination with biblical texts and the poetry of Omar Khayyam and William Blake.

PINEAPPLE, DUNMORE, SCOTLAND

LEFT, RIGHT AND PAGE 28 What possessed the honorable John Murray, 4th Earl of Dunmore, to crown his existing Palladian hothouse with a 37 foot (11 meter) high stone pineapple has baffled his descendants and architectural historians alike. Its domed masonry foliage forms the roof to a hexagonal cupola whose Gothic windows provide natural light to a small banqueting hall beneath. It is possible that one of the exotic delicacies served in these opulent surroundings was the inspiration behind this act of architectural bravado as records confirm that pineapples were grown against the heated hothouse walls, although at no small expense. The rarity and exclusiveness of tropical fruit in 18th-century Europe made the pineapple a natural symbol of wealth and power, and it was frequently used in applied arts, appearing on wallpapers, moldings, silverware and decorative stonework. The Pineapple has been carefully prepared (as a weekend retreat) and can now be rented for short vacations through the Landmark Trust. Perfect for a fruity weekend.

THE ROYAL PAVILION, BRIGHTON, SUSSEX, ENGLAND

RIGHT AND PAGES 30–31 Situated in the resort of Brighton, southern England, the Royal Pavilion was originally the seaside retreat of the heir to the British throne, George, Prince of Wales, in the 1780s. He became prince regent in 1815 and employed leading architect Thomas Nash to transform the site of the existing Palladian villa into something altogether more exotic. Nash created a unique style for George, one known as Oriental-Gothic, and came up with a flamboyant exterior concoction of Indian and Chinese architecture with domes, minarets and pagodas, all supported by a cutting-edge cast-iron frame. The pavilion's interior is equally exotic, featuring dragons, palm trees and bamboo work.

THE NEEDLE'S EYE, WENTWORTH WOODHOUSE, ENGLAND

This folly lies within the grounds of Wentworth Woodhouse estate, in the West Riding of Yorkshire, and was probably built in the mid-18th century under the orders of the Second Marquis of Rockingham, then one of the country's richest men. It consists of a sandstone pyramid some 45 feet (14 meters) high, topped by an ornamental funerary urn that is pierced by a narrow Gothic ogee arch a little under 9 feet (3 meters) wide. Legend has it that Rockingham had the structure built over an old private road on the estate to win a wager that he could drive a coach and horses through the eye of a needle.

UPTURNED BOAT SHEDS, LINDISFARNE, ENGLAND

LEFT Clinging to the rugged Northumbrian Coast, Holy Island can claim to have played host to more than 450 years of recycling, since Henry VIII first ordered the stones of the dissolved Lindisfarne Priory to be removed to build a new artillery fort. Perched upon the rocky Beblowe Crag, it defended the exposed Lindisfarne harbor from attack until the union of England and Scotland under James I rendered it redundant. Over the centuries it slowly decayed until being bought in 1901 by Edward Hudson, founder of *Country Life* magazine. Hudson had fallen in love with the island's romantic isolation and commissioned architect Sir Edwin Lutyens in 1903 to transform the ruined fort into a lavish weekend retreat. In addition to converting Hudson's castle into a home, Lutyens chose to add three garden huts on the grounds by recycling the upturned hulls of local herring boats and waterproofing them with sailcloth and bitumen — a knowing architectural nod to the maritime history of the area. Two of the three huts were destroyed by fire in 2005, but they have since been replaced using another herring boat and the hull of a pilot's lighter, continuing the island's legacy of reclamation into the 21st century.

BIG DUCK, FLANDERS, NEW YORK, NY

RIGHT This fine example of U.S. roadside architecture near Flanders, at the eastern end of New York State's Long Island, was created by duck farmer Martin Maurer in 1931. He set to work using ferrocement over a wooden frame and used the headlights of a Model T Ford for the eyes, which glowed red at night. The final structure measures 20 feet (6 meters) tall by 30 feet (9 meters) long and was hollow so that Maurer could sell eggs to passersby from its belly. The duck has been moved several times but is now watched over by a preservation society and is used to sell souvenirs to weekending New Yorkers and other visitors.

TRIANGULAR LODGE, RUSHTON, NORTHAMPTONSHIRE, ENGLAND

Sir Thomas Tresham was a staunch supporter of the Catholic faith, which was a dangerous position in Protestant Elizabethan England, yet he chose to celebrate his religious beliefs by building a lodge on the grounds of Rushton Hall, Northamptonshire, in the 1590s. The construction was based on the number three, to symbolize the Holy Trinity, so the lodge has three sides of 33 feet (the age that Jesus Christ is thought to have been when he died), three floors and three triangular gables on each side. Each floor also has three windows, and each window has a threefold trefoil design. Even the central chimney has three sides.

SCHLOSS NEUSCHWANSTEIN, BAVARIA, GERMANY

LEFT, RIGHT AND PAGES 40–41 This fairy-tale granite castle in southern Bavaria, Germany, was the obsession of King Ludwig II, a spendthrift supporter of art and architecture. Ludwig wanted to make tangible his divine right to rule, the chivalric code of medieval Germany and the works of composer Richard Wagner, who flourished under his patronage. Plans for the castle were drawn up by the king and a theater designer, Christian Jank, and work began in 1869 under the supervision of trained architects. The castle exhibits a variety of styles — Byzantine, Gothic and Romanesque — but it was never actually completed. Ludwig was declared insane in 1886 and drowned in mysterious circumstances the same year.

RESIDENTIAL BUILDINGS

HUNDERTWASSER-HAUS, VIENNA, AUSTRIA

Born Friedrich Stowasser to a Jewish family in Vienna on December 15, 1928, Friedensreich Hundertwasser is probably Austria's best-known artist. His pictorial works were original, unruly and shocking, inspired by the works of Egon Schiele and compared with that of Gustav Klimt. His adopted surname is based on the translation of *Sto*, the Czech word for *Hundert*, which is German for hundred. "Friedensreich" means peace-land. Today his renown comes from his buildings — such as the Hundertwasserhaus (**LEFT, RIGHT, AND PAGES 46–47**), a low-income apartment block in Vienna featuring undulating floors. Also illustrated is (**FAR RIGHT**) the incinerator in Vienna, the outside of the buildings of which he turned into a totally unique work of art.

HABITAT '67, MONTREAL, CANADA

Built as part of the Montreal Expo in 1967 and based directly upon his master's thesis, Moshe Safdie's Habitat '67 housing complex is quite literally an essay in concrete. At a casual glance the development looks to be entirely random, but all 158 apartments share a common DNA in the identical concrete cubes that form the basic unit of the cellular structure. Safdie combined 354 of these prefabricated components in groups ranging from one to eight to create 15 different sizes of apartments, ensuring that it could cater to a wide range of residential needs, from single people to families, forming a balanced community. This was a proactive interpretation of the Expo's overriding theme, "Man and His World," in which architecture shapes man's environment, acting as a form of a benign social engineering. As is so often the case, Safdie's utopian ideals did not fare well in the commercial world, and despite the extensive use of prefabricated components, the system proved to be prohibitively expensive. The final irony it that this experimental model for mass social housing has become an exclusive, privately owned condominium with 24-hour concierge service.

SPACESHIP HOUSE, SYDNEY, NEW SOUTH WALES, AUSTRALIA

LEFT, RIGHT AND PAGE 52 In 1963, 10 years before the complex concrete shells of the Sydney Opera House were finally completed, maverick architect Eugene Van Grecken was putting the finishing touches to his own home, just 40 minutes' drive away in Bayview. Although more modest in scale, his house was no less daring, boasting what was then the largest freeform concrete structure in the southern hemisphere. His Spaceship House derives its name from its elliptical domed concrete roof, some 83 feet by 68 feet (25 meters by 20 meters) across, which rests upon 11 boomerang-shaped pillars. Amazingly, this colossal carapace, pierced by two rings of circular skylights, is held on only by gravity. It rests upon 2 inch (5 cm) thick neoprene pads on the pillars' tips that allow it to slide back and forth as it expands and contracts in the fierce heat of the Australian sun. Seated in the open-plan interior, like James Bond villains in a theatrical lair, residents can gaze down the precipitous cliff side at the sailing boats bobbing some 502 feet (153 meters) below.

BUILDING WITH A HOLE, REPULSE BAY, HONG KONG

RIGHT Beautiful Repulse Bay is situated on the southern coast of Hong Kong Island and is popular with both locals and visitors. It consists of a broad curving beach, backed by steep-sloped mountains. Because of land shortages, modern architects have had to build upward to offset spiraling costs. The bay was home to the colonial-style Repulse Bay Hotel until the early 1980s, when it was replaced by this large apartment block that has a large square hole cut through its structure. This was supposedly done because in Chinese mythology, a dragon, largely placid but easily irritated, lives in every mountain and needs an uninterrupted view of the sea to remain benevolent.

HERNANDEZ HOUSE, BOSQUES DE LAS LOMAS, MEXICO

A stunning exercise in geometrical gymnastics, Casa Hernández is one Mexican architect's response to the challenge of building on a precipitous slope. With the few remaining level plots in the suburb of Mexico City commanding a high premium, Agustín Hérnandez chose to reclaim the full depth of his site by making his building leap into the air. Approached from the hillside road, the house appears like a prismatic space cruiser from the cult film "Tron," lightly tethered to the rocky gradient. Two upright walls, 115 feet (35 meters) high, are pierced by four prisms held captive within circular apertures cast into the uprights. Supported by massive beams, the prisms seem to be sliding past each other, imparting a kinetic quality to the structure but also creating a projecting balcony at the front and a covered parking space at the rear. The interior is dominated by a seam of glazing that runs up the full height of the facade, taking full advantage of the house's commanding position. Residents are treated to a twinkling nocturnal vista after sunset.

CASA AMALIA, MEXICO

When Agustín Hérnandez designed this house for his sister, Amalia, in 1969, he sought to capture the essence of her graceful profession and fix it in the third dimension. A talented choreographer, Amalia founded Mexico City's Ballet Folklórico in 1952. Under her inspired guidance it flourished, going on to represent Mexico at the Pan American Games of 1959. The main staircase seems like an echo of the rising, sweeping spirals described by the ruffled skirts of the ballet's twirling Latin dancers, while every beam and lintel appears to mirror the arching curves of performers at full stretch. But there is a second layer of narrative here. The curving plain white rendered walls and subdued palette of natural materials refer back to the humble Hispanic monasteries in the area, an oasis of cloistered tranquillity to return to after the drama of the stage. The whole piece is given a honey-colored hue by a round skylight set into a small tilted dome, glazed with a translucent slab of veined onyx, as though the daylight is being filtered through the delicate tissue of a seductively batted eyelid. Amalia died in 2000, but her daughter Viviana, also a choreographer, continues to live in the family home, keeping the building's spirit alive.

CUBIC HOUSES, ROTTERDAM, THE NETHERLANDS

Like Moshe Safdie, Dutch architect Piet Blom strove to achieve a sense of community through architecture, to unite people by creating village environments within a larger city context. "Living under an urban roof" was how he described his approach, and with the Kubuswoning (Cubic Houses) of 1984 he translated this philosophy into a dazzling geometric grove of 38 dwellings, in an abstract composition worthy of a cubist painter. The tree analogy is not entirely superficial as the cubes' faces are constructed from timber frames clad in cement and wood fiberboard panels, with the roofs being sheathed in wooden shingles. Each house has a "trunk" composed of three concrete pillars surrounded by a hexagonal brick wall shell, above which are three reinforced concrete floor plates that act as "branches." As the cubes have been balanced on their corners, the first and third of the three floors are triangular, with windows sharply inclined toward the street or the sky. Each "tree" reaches out to touch its neighbor, providing mutual structural support and presenting passing planes with continuous forest canopy. Blom succeeded in creating an arboreal urban community, encouraging man to take to the trees once more.

CYCLOPS SOUND WALL HOUSES, DIEPENDAAL, THE NETHERLANDS

As they pass through the woods of Hilversum, on the busy road from Diependaal, many drivers ignore the light green polycarbonate edging the shoulder, a mere flickering burr in their peripheral vision. From their moving cars this is the only outward sign of a cunning residential project buttressing the earth of the embankment. The 12 Cyclops Sound Wall houses poke out of the soil, like a gigantic saw-toothed blade, cutting down the rumble of the passing traffic by supporting the polycarbonate sound barrier at their backs. The barrier brings the ambient noise down to an acceptable level for the houses opposite, while the Cyclops residents themselves are assured of a good night's sleep in their ground floor bedrooms, well-insulated well below road level. Above their brick-built lower walls soar the cantilevered aluminum-clad living spaces with their single full-width windows (the Cyclops' eye), a gravity-defying touch made possible by anchoring the structure in the mass of the embankment. Living in houses designed to deaden noise pollution for others may seem like a saintly, selfless act, but when you look at the quality of Maurice Nio's elegant solution it hardly seems like a sacrifice at all.

CASA BATLLO, BARCELONA, SPAIN

Located at 43 Passeig de Gràcia (*passeig* is Catalan for promenade or avenue) in the Eixample district of Barcelona, Casa Batllo was designed by architect Antoni Gaudi, whose best-known work is Barcelona's unfinished Sagrada Familia cathedral (see pages 216–17). Designed and built at the peak of the art nouveau movement in 1905–1907, Casa Batllo is very much of its period, with its sinuous — almost organic — lines, none of which get anywhere close to straight. The second house Gaudi designed on this street (the other is La Pedrera), Batllo was built for Josep Batllo, a wealthy aristocrat, as a townhouse. He and his family lived in the lower two floors and the upper floors were rented out as apartments.

The photographs here and on pages 64–65 show the facade (**LEFT AND PAGE 64**), balcony (**BELOW**) and roof (**RIGHT**) details, and the fabulous interior (**PAGE 65**). Casa Batllo was included in UNESCO's World Heritage Listing in July 2005.

TWISTING TORSO HIGH-RISE APARTMENT TOWER, MALMÖ, SWEDEN

Situated in Malmö, Sweden, overlooking the Oresund Strait, the Twisting Torso was created by Spanish-born architect Santiago Calatrava at the behest of the local branch of a cooperative housing association (HSB). It was inspired by one of Calatrava's own sculptures, The Twisting Torso, which had been seen by a senior HSB member and consists of a 623-foot (190-meter) tower of nine five-story blocks that twist as they rise, with the uppermost being aligned at 90 degrees to the lowest. The building, which has won numerous awards, contains offices in the lower blocks and 149 luxury apartments in those above, along with various panorama rooms.

SHARK IN A HOUSE
HEADINGTON, OXFORD, ENGLAND

LEFT The Shark became the most famous resident of Headington when it landed in the roof of 2 New High Street on August 9, 1986. This ordinary suburban home was owned then (as it is today) by American Bill Heine, who studied law at Balliol College, Oxford, commissioned the shark and still owns the house. Since 1988 he has been better known as a Radio Oxford presenter. When pressed by journalists to provide a rationale for the shark, he suggested:

> The shark was to express someone feeling totally impotent and ripping a hole in their roof out of a sense of impotence and anger and desperation ... It is saying something about CND, nuclear power, Chernobyl and Nagasaki.

Created by sculptor John Buckley, it is made of fiberglass, weighs 450 pounds (200 kg) and is 25 feet (7.5 meters) long. The local authorities tried to force Heine to get rid rid of the shark, so finally, in 1991, Heine appealed to the secretary of state for the environment (then Michael Heseltine), and in 1992 Heseltine came out in favor of the shark.

FIVE SPHINXES APARTMENT BUILDINGS, HUIZEN, THE NETHERLANDS

RIGHT AND PAGES 70–71 Considering their precarious position on the lowlands of Europe, it is perhaps unsurprising that it is the Dutch who have learned not only to live with water but also to dwell upon it. This act of architectural defiance toward the encroaching waters is typical of the adventurous spirit that pervades the Netherlands, making them by far the most progressive EU country in terms of modern residential schemes. Arrayed like powerful swimmers straining on their starting blocks, the Five Sphinxes jut out into Gooimeer Lake, ready to take the plunge. Their wedge-like aluminum-clad forms are the result of each successive floor having one less apartment than the last (14 in each "sphinx"), climaxing in twin penthouses that divide the "heads" down the centerline.

Their sloping "backs," warmed by the sun, contain sunken roof-terraces for six apartments, while another four boast waterside balconies that nestle under the overhanging "chins." The residents' private parking lots are actually underwater in the submerged foundation tanks, accessed via the ramps that link the sphinxes to the shore. All that seems to be missing is an airlock from which to launch private submersibles into the lake's blue waters.

HOUSE IN THE CLOUDS, THORPENESS, SUFFOLK, ENGLAND

LEFT This structure is part of the mock-Tudor coastal village of Thorpeness, on the Suffolk coast in eastern England, which was created in the early 20th century by Glencairn Stuart Ogilvie, an architect, barrister and playwright of Scottish descent. His aim was to provide a holiday resort for the affluent middle class — especially their children — that captured the spirit of "Merrie England." It also took inspiration from *Peter Pan*, as the book's author, J. M. Barrie, was a family friend. The five-story House in the Clouds was originally built in 1926 to enclose an unsightly water tank, but the latter was subsequently removed when centrally supplied water arrived. The house now offers holiday accommodation.

THE JUNGLE, LINCOLNSHIRE, ENGLAND

RIGHT If the traditional folly is meant to represent the eccentricity of its owner, then The Jungle in Eagle may be the perfect personification of its original patron. Some time in the 1820s Samuel Russell Collett commissioned architect Thomas Lovely to create a hybrid home, half redbrick farmhouse, half rusticated folly, to serve as a suitably bizarre backdrop to his collection of exotic animals. American deer, kangaroos, pheasants and buffalo numbered among his personal menagerie, and all were permitted to wander freely around the grounds, no doubt to the alarm of the unsuspecting visitor. As befits a folly, even the materials employed were a facsimile of the real thing. Burnt bricks, the inevitable wastage created by the inconsistent heat of contemporary brick kilns, were substituted for weathered medieval stone. In the process Lovely created a pleasingly textured facade that provided countless toe holds for the Leylandii and ivy that have since colonized the exterior. His treatment of the doors and windows was equally artificial, but no less picturesque. The crude, rough-hewn timber frames of the pointed Gothic windows complement a leaf-shaped front door that would not look out of place in J. R. R. Tolkein's Hobbiton. Now a Grade II listed folly, the house was dramatically extended in the late 1970s to become a palatial seven-bedroom mansion whose bulk is still disguised by Collett's ivy-clad original.

TSUI HOUSE, BERKELEY, CA

Like the shell of some prehistoric creature washed up in a Californian suburb, the house Dr. Eugene Tsui designed for his parents is in sharp contrast to its rectilinear neighbors. This suggestion of the sea is no coincidence as Tsui's inspiration was the tardigrade, a hardy microscopic marine invertebrate capable of living in almost any environment in the world, from the Arctic to the tropics. With walls made from recycled Styrofoam and cement, and a curving roof built up from layers of stress wood sheeting sprayed with concrete, the house is both highly insulated and practically earthquake proof. The final layer of heavily textured gold-painted render hides a further innovation; a series of black plastic pipes filled with water that absorb the heat of the sun's rays by day and radiate it back into the house at night. The portholed tower, rising above the cooling fins like a Victorian diver's helmet, contains the master bedroom, but residents can find cooler sanctuary in the living room at the base of the central rotunda, cocooned by the spiraling ramp. The accretion of unconventional materials, applied in layers with bucket and trowel, makes the Tsui House within the reach of the ambitious self-builder wanting an organic way out of the wasteland of white boxes.

XANADU HOUSE FOR THE FUTURE, KISSIMMEE, FL

LEFT A collaboration between architect Roy Mason and inventor Bob Masters, the Xanadu House at Kissimmee offered a glimpse of a future that has not come to pass. The experimental "home of tomorrow" attracted more than 1,000 visitors a day when it first opened its doors in 1983, with its unconventional construction methods and the high level of integrated computer technology, at a time when home computing was still in its infancy. The house's highly organic cellular form was achieved by using an inflated 40-foot-wide vinyl balloon as a reusable mold, a 5-inch layer of quick-drying polyurethane foam being sprayed onto its interior surface, creating a series of white living pods. Connecting corridors were fabricated from expanded wire mesh, also sprayed with foam, resulting in a house that had the appearance of a molecular atomic diagram made out of marshmallows. The nuclear family of the future was to have the latest information technology at its disposal, a built-in programmable central computer controlling everything from heating and lighting to monitoring the contents of the refrigerator. This level of IT intrusion is still being prototyped in the private mansion of Microsoft billionaire Bill Gates, but for mainstream America the Xanadu House proved to be less-than-desirable and visitor numbers declined before it was finally demolished in 2005.

HIGH DESERT HOUSE, PALM SPRINGS, CA

RIGHT AND PAGES 78–79 Instead of ordering his arid, boulder-strewn desert site to be cleared, architect Kendrick Bangs Kellogg chose to create a house that responded to the topography of the landscape, neatly slotting his concrete interventions among the jostling boulders. Blending with its surroundings, the house appears to flow down the hillside, its 26 overlapping concrete leaves forming a herringbone-patterned shell of arching sunshades. Each shade is an independent element, rooted 7 feet (2 meters) into the natural rock, and capable of swaying gently to absorb the force of the tremors should an earthquake strike. Between each concrete leaf, windows of tempered glass are set in rubberized gaskets to accommodate the movements caused by aftershocks. The interior is no less dramatic, the living space being dominated by the "dragon's tail," a spiraling tendril of rusted steel vertebrae that support glass-topped workstations for the graphic designers who commissioned the beast. Every surface and component is custom-made, crafted in bronze and steel, pebble mosaic and etched glass. It may have taken Kellogg and artisan John Vugrin more than 15 years to create, but the result is truly a 21st-century "*Gesamtkunstwerk*" — quite literally "a total work of art."

SUN VALLEY HOUSE, ID

LEFT, RIGHT AND PAGES 82–84 Like a landscape in miniature, the undulating curves of the Sun Valley House echo the surrounding hills as it nestles in the shadow of its natural environment. Its unusual rippling plan of four interlocking volumes was designed as a direct response to the client's desire for both guests and residents to have a degree of privacy during their stay. Architect Bart Prince's solution was to place the semicircular bedrooms in separate wings, facing in opposite directions, and linked to a central living space by a spinal corridor. At each extremity of the building this corridor transforms into half-round external passageways, ribbed with steel and planked with fir, like landlocked ships' hulls or medieval castle hoardings. While the bedrooms are roofed in wooden shingles, the central living rooms are sheathed in twisting copper vertebrae holding skylights that frame the view of the stars at night. The house sits on raised concrete foundations, anticipating the thick snows of winter and waist-high grasses of summer that would have otherwise obscured the views down the valley. The house may look like a Tolkien-esque fantasy, but it has been perfectly designed to allow uninterrupted enjoyment of the wonders of the real natural world.

EGYPTIAN HOUSE, PENZANCE, ENGLAND

RIGHT Chapel Street in the picturesque fishing community of Penzance, Cornwall, in far southwest England, is home to a rare surviving example of the craze for all things Ancient Egyptian that swept the country following Napoleon Bonaparte's expedition to Egypt in the late 18th century. A Cornish mineralogist, John Lavin, commissioned a designer, possibly John Foulston of nearby Plymouth, to construct a building with an ornate facade that is thought to have been inspired by the Temple of Hathor at Dendra in Egypt. The building used coade artificial stone (a mix of crushed stone and clay) and was Lavin's home until his death, whereupon it was sold by his son.

PRINCE HOUSE, ALBUQUERQUE, NM

Turning a corner in a quiet quarter of Albuquerque, the casual passerby is confronted by a floating form, a fir-colored UFO with an array of dark porthole eyes gazing down on them from among the treetops. This is the home and studio of architect Bart Prince, an "organic" architect par excellence. Like so many architects, Prince has used his own house as a testing ground for his ideas, and within this relatively modest structure can be discerned forms and themes that reappear in his later work for wealthy patrons. Standing tall on a series of four concrete towers, the most distinctive element to his careful composition is the long lozenge-shaped volume, its rounded sides clad in fir planks over steel ribs, reminiscent of a wooden ship's hull. The maritime theme continues with the eight hooded round portholes, arrayed in a semi-circle at one end to give the house its "face." The effect is at once futuristic and medieval; an object out of sync with its time, akin to Leonardo Da Vinci's sketchy designs for a timber Renaissance tank, or a Jules Verne submersible. Whatever the interpretation, Prince's house is an outstanding vehicle for his ideas.

CHEMOSPHERE HOUSE, ABOVE LOS ANGELES, CA

A protégé of Frank Lloyd Wright's Taliesin School, John Lautner was not a man to be deterred by a 45-degree sloping site and a tight budget. His solution was a single concrete pillar, 5 feet (1.5 meters) thick and 27 feet (8 meters) tall, a slender stem from which flowered an octagonal house that floated like some faceted flying saucer. The press was quick to make such comparisons,

the Chemosphere having descended upon Los Angeles just three years after Sputnik's launch, but the house's appearance was not stylistic affectation but a genuine example of innovative problem solving. The futuristic steel envelope hides older technology, the major structural components being made from laminated wood, previously used by Lautner's engineer, John de la Vaux, to build boats. Their client, Leonard Malin, was an aircraft engineer, and his profession provided further inspiration when it came to ventilating his new home.

Perched on its mast the house exposes its underside to the sky, with discreet angled vents drawing air up through the double-walled sides. It emerges behind the slanting glass windows and through natural convection rises along the curved lines of the ceiling to be expelled through the Plexiglas dome at the top. A true machine for living, the house effectively draws air through itself like a jet engine.

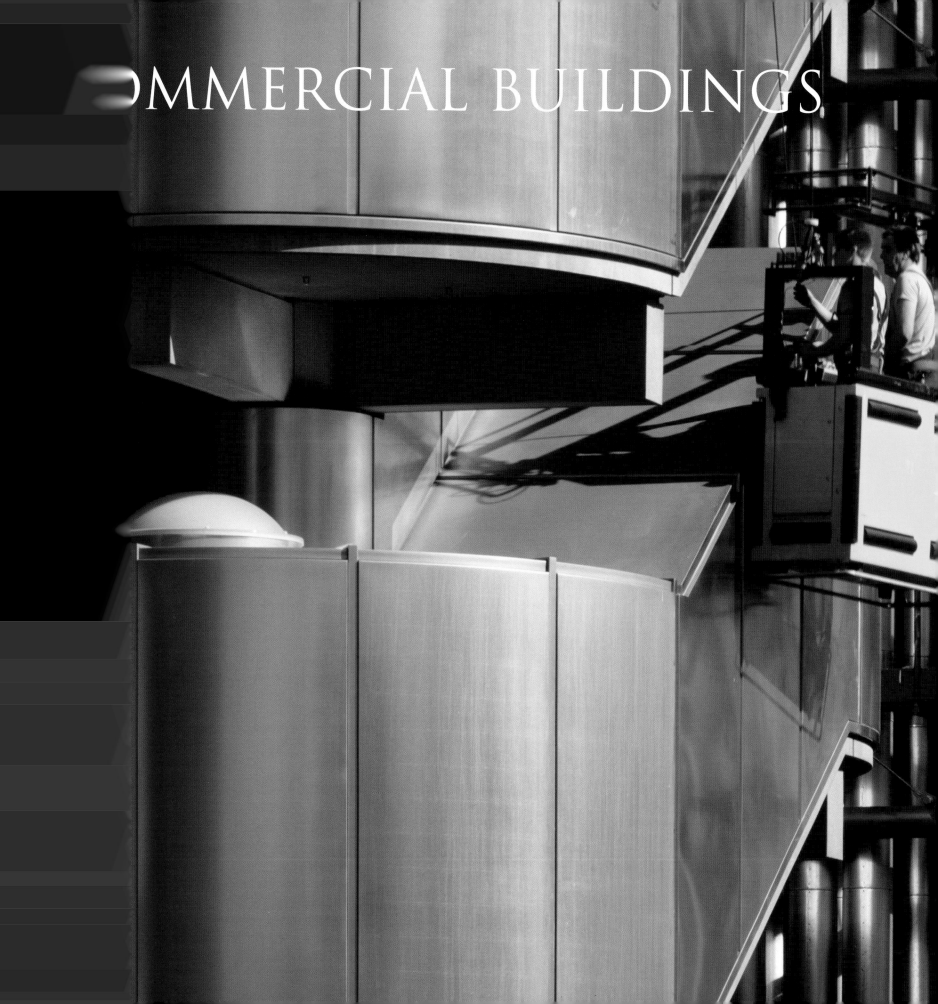

OMMERCIAL BUILDINGS

ORIENTAL PEARL TV TOWER, SHANGHAI, CHINA

This concrete-and-steel monument to rapidly modernizing China was built in bustling Shanghai's Pudong New Area between July 1991 and October 1994 and was officially opened the following year. It was designed by Jia Huan Cheng of the Shanghai Modern Architecture Design Company and was based on a similar building in Berlin. The tower rises to 1,536 feet (468 meters), making it the tallest structure in Asia and the third tallest in the world. It consists of a series of slanting columns and spheres of various sizes and is a truly multifunctional complex with entertainment and hotel facilities, history and science museums, as well as bars and restaurants and viewing platforms.

BURJ AL ARAB HOTEL, DUBAI

RIGHT, FAR RIGHT, AND PAGES 96–97 Dubai's Burj Al Arab is a beacon for the ambition of a Gulf state that has blossomed from preindustrial backwater to international player in less than half a century. The tallest hotel in world, the 1,053-foot (321-meter) tower was commissioned by the late Sheikh Maktoum bin Rashid Al Maktoum with the express purpose of creating a readily identifiable icon to complete his vision for Dubai. It stands apart from the city on its own manmade island and similarly distances itself from its competitors by claiming to be the world's only seven-star luxury hotel. An architectural interpretation of the billowing spinnakers of passing luxury yachts and traditional dhows, the structure's curved side is skinned in a Teflon-veneered glass-fiber fabric that acts as a high-tech sunshade. Its cooling influence is essential as the desert sun would quickly transform the impressive 590-foot (180-meter) atrium into a solar furnace, perhaps melting the 8,000 square meters of 22-carat gold leaf that give the cigar-shaped columns their Flash Gordon glamor. Like a lofty crow's nest pinned to the hotel's masthead, the cantilevered crosspiece contains the Al Muntaha restaurant, from which diners can gaze far out to sea. The enlarged circuit-board motifs that adorn its walls are suitably symbolic of the way Dubai has adapted Western technology to meet its own decorative and economic needs.

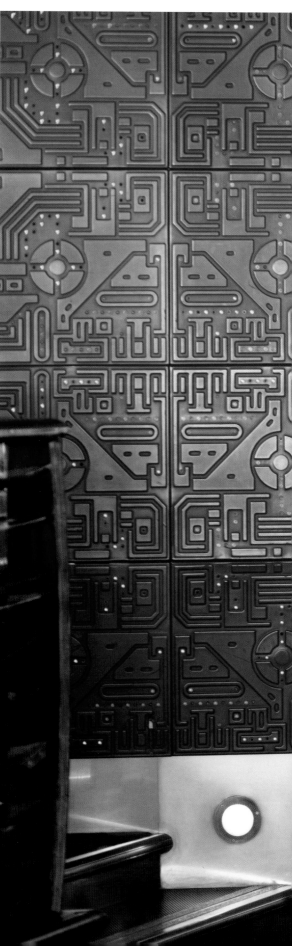

LLOYDS BUILDING, LONDON, ENGLAND

LEFT, RIGHT AND PAGE 100 The epitome of 80s Britain, Lloyds of London is a true engine of commerce, its exterior glittering with an accretion of pipes and services that have been banished from the trading floors, leaving more room for the moneymen of the markets to do their work. This was Richard Rogers' first major commission after the phenomenally successful Centre Pompidou and a continuation of its dominating theme of open-plan, flexible space. The building that Rogers first envisioned was intended as a cathedral of light, with delicate service towers acting like high-tech flying buttresses, ringing the barrel-vaulted atrium. However, the rapid growth in office computers and numbers of traders demanded far more power and air-conditioning, forcing the design to evolve. The delicate buttresses swelled to become the massive, fortress-like towers we see today, crowned by the boxes of plant and machinery. The marble-run-like staircase capsules and stainless steel toilet pods that give this engine its dramatic cooling fins were all prefabricated off-site and craned into place, saving both time and money. And yet in the midst of all this 20th-century engineering stands a mahogany classical cupola, containing the famous *Lutine* Bell, recovered from the wreck of the *Lutine* in 1858. Its ominous single ring portends the loss of a ship and an insurance claim that must honored. The pinstriped suits may have helped build a new world order, but they haven't forgotten their history.

TODS OMOTESANDO BUILDING, TOKYO, JAPAN

RIGHT Stimulated by the economic success of the iconic Guggenheim Bilbao, it wasn't long before the world of fashion joined the race to create lucrative new signature buildings. Keen to associate their designer collections with the cream of the architectural community, Prada teamed up with Herzog & De Meuron, Armani courted Tadao Ando and accessories brand Tod's sought the vision of Toyo Ito. Ito's concept for their flagship Tokyo store employed the natural forms of the Zelkova trees that lined the fashionable boulevard of Omotesando, making a very direct link between building and its context. The abstracted silhouettes of nine different trees were combined to create a lattice pattern of tapering concrete members, which act as both structure and facade, leaving the interior open and largely column-free. The facade is especially dramatic in the late evening when the sunset transforms the gray concrete planes into warm orange trunks, expressing the graphic quality of Ito's design as an angular woodcut, printed on the city's skyline. Allowing the architect to design both exterior and interior resulted in a seamless continuity, the tree-like branches being continued in the few interior walls, creating unusual room dividers that deepen the illusion of arboreal bargain hunting.

FUJI SANKEI BUILDING, TOKYO, JAPAN

Rising 25 stories out of the artificial island of Odaiba, the Fuji Sankei Headquarters Building has become synonymous with its occupants, an essential part of their corporate iconography. After the first four floors, the structure splits into two separate towers linked by an immensely strong web of hollow box girder walkways that brace them against the shock of Japan's frequent earthquakes. Caught in this net of aluminum conduits sits a gigantic titanium-clad sphere, 105 feet (32 meters) in diameter, its aircraft warning beacon flashing like the timer on an immense thermal detonator. This unexpected "eye" gives the building its distinctive silhouette, the interior being divided into three to form a domed observation platform over a restaurant and a machine room. If the overall aesthetic seems akin to some mechanistic molecular diagram it is due to architect Kenzo Tange's close relationship with the Metabolist group, which sought to design buildings that could evolve and adapt to meet changing needs by mimicking microscopic biological processes such as the accumulation and reduction of cells in tissue. The gaping voids left between the walkways suggest that this really is a building capable of inward regeneration.

NAKAGIN CAPSULE TOWER, TOKYO, JAPAN

Despite being a significant structure in the history of Metabolist architecture, the Nakagin Capsule Tower is actually in danger of demolition, thanks to more than 30 years of neglect. Architect Kisho Kurokawa's original design concept treated the 140 compact pods as an outer layer of living cells that would be periodically "shed" to allow the building to be "regenerated," mimicking the life cycle of our own skin. To this end each of the 13 x 8 foot (4 x 2.5 meter) capsules was designed to be easily craned into position and fastened to the concrete core towers, with just four high-tension bolts apiece. The ingenious interiors feel like domesticated lunar modules, with folding beds, built-in bathrooms and integrated entertainment consoles. The high degree of structural flexibility meant that the capsules could be swapped around to create new configurations, some forming mini-offices and studios, whereas others became overnight accommodation for businessmen obliged to work long hours. In theory, groups of capsules could even be linked together to create homes for entire families. If only the owners had stuck to Kurokawa's plan and periodically shuffled their pack of pods, then the current residents might not be campaigning so vociferously to have their capsules dismantled for good.

GOETHEANUM BOILER HOUSE, DOERN, SWITZERLAND

LEFT Located in Dornach, Switzerland, the Goetheanum is home to the country's anthroposophical movement, a spiritual-religious philosophy, and is named after Johann Wolfgang Goethe, the famed German poet, author and philosopher. It has had two incarnations. The First Goetheanum was a wooden structure built between 1913 and 1919 as designed by Austrian-born social philosopher Rudolph Steiner, the movement's founder. This structure was destroyed in an arson attack on New Year's Eve 1922–1923. Steiner, who died in 1925, designed the Second Goetheanum in concrete, cast into intricate patterns. It was built between 1924 and 1928. The building contains a 1,000-seat auditorium and now has protected status.

MEDIUM MARKET BASKET, DRESDEN, OHIO

RIGHT The Longaberger Company is a maker of hand-crafted maple wood baskets. It is one of the primary employers in the southeastern Ohio area near Dresden. Started in Dresden, the company is now headquartered in Newark, Ohio. A family-owned and operated business, the Longaberger Company was started by Dave Longaberger and after his death is now owned by daughters Tami Longaberger and Rachel Longaberger. The Longaberger corporate headquarters on Ohio State Highway 16 is a local landmark and a well-known example of novelty architecture since it takes the shape of their biggest seller, the "Medium Market Basket." Originally, Dave Longaberger wanted all of the Longaberger buildings to be shaped like baskets, but only the headquarters was completed by his death. After his death, further basket-shaped buildings were vetoed by his daughters.

TORRE AGBAR, BARCELONA, SPAIN

LEFT, RIGHT AND PAGES 110–11 A glittering glass geyser has erupted onto the skyline of Gaudi's Barcelona, a modern incarnation of that architect's love of fractured, dappled colors and irregular pattern. The aquatic metaphor was quite deliberate as French architect Jean Nouvel designed the tower at the bequest of the Catalonian water company Aguas de Barcelona. The 466-foot (144-meter) structure has two concrete shells: an outer hull perforated with some 4,500 individually cut windows and an inner core that contains most of the lifts and services. This inner core functions as a single, gigantic, load-bearing column that allows the office floors to be entirely open plan. The outer shell ends five stories from the top, the final floors being simply cantilevered from the extended inner core and wrapped in the steel and glass nose cone that forms the tower's climax. What gives the tower its chameleon-like quality are the brightly colored aluminum panels that clad the concrete hull, so lightweight that they flex in the prevailing breeze, causing the whole skin to shimmer. They peer from behind a suspended facade of 56,619 transparent and translucent glass louvers, computer controlled to modulate the glare and solar gain. In a final theatrical touch Nouvel added 4,500 pink, blue and red lights so that his preening peacock could continue to court the city by night.

SWISS RE BUILDING, LONDON, ENGLAND

LEFT, RIGHT AND PAGES 114–15 Compared with the Torre Agbar, with its heavy concrete core disguised with glass and aluminum, Swiss RE is an honest expression of engineering intent. Its sleek ballistic exterior is a rigid exoskeleton that acts as both facade and structure, achieving the same light, open-plan interiors as its Spanish counterpart but with far greater economy. This drive for efficiency forms the core of Norman Foster and Partners' design, the entire building being geared to minimizing energy consumption, particularly in terms of light and heat. At 590 feet (180 meters) tall with 41 floors, each circular level is divided into six radiating fingers, leaving six triangular-shaped voids in between. The standard floor plan is then rotated on each successive level, linking these voids together to form the distinctive twisting black-glazed spirals, like rifled grooves on an immense artillery projectile. These are the lungs of the building, drawing fresh air spiraling up the tower using only natural convection, contributing to an overall energy saving of up to 50%. A fitting reward for such an eco-conscious investment is the fully glazed occupant's only restaurant in the rocket's "nose cone," a column-free vantage point from which to survey the city of London.

SELFRIDGES, BIRMINGHAM, ENGLAND

Poised as if preparing to devour the shoals of shoppers that flow across its curving footbridge, the new Selfridges store looms over Birmingham like a creature from the blue lagoon. Its reptilian skin is a glittering array of more than 15,000 anodized aluminum disks bolted to an undulating facade of sprayed concrete rendered over contoured layers of expanded steel mesh. Future Systems' inspiration is said to have come from the shimmering chain-mail dresses of designer Paco Rabanne, combining chic fashion statement with shock value structure to inject the Selfridges brand with some much-needed adrenaline. The monolithic blue bulk of the exterior is coated in Monolastex, a durable liquid plastic normally used for painting lighthouses, which should give many more years of wear than the average impulse purchase. Inside, the architects drove a vast tapering atrium down through the center of the building, whose progressively wider openings draw natural light into every floor. The void is crisscrossed by sleek futuristic escalators, whose white fiberglass and reinforced plaster-clad curves appear to morph seamlessly into the walls. With this sense of every element being organically molded from the same block of plasticine, it is easy to understand why the "style" has been christened "blobitecture."

TRINITY BUOY WHARF, LONDON, ENGLAND

Like a child's stack of technicolored Lego bricks, the 30 recycled shipping containers of Trinity Buoy Wharf are a playful and innovative solution to the needs of London's community of artists and craftspeople. With the growing trend for converting the capital's once-plentiful old factories and warehouses into exclusive loft apartments, the traditional source of cheap studio space was drying up. A group of developers, Urban Space Management, made the decision to create purpose-built workshops on a budget. The 8 foot (2.5 m) square by 78 foot (24 m) long containers provided incredibly strong basic building blocks with which to experiment, the corrugated metal skins potentially permitting stacks up to 10 units high. The maritime character of the containers was maintained by the cutting of circular porthole-shaped windows, while welding the end doors open to form balconies further contributed to the structural rigidity and consistent appearance. Inside, some of the containers have had their inner walls removed, creating studios of varying sizes. The speed of construction and use of recycled elements helped keep costs down, enabling Urban Space Management to quite literally "Pile 'em high and let 'em cheap!"

CHIAT/DAY BUILDING, VENICE, CA

LEFT Main Street, Venice, California, and what could be more unexpected than a giant pair of binoculars in the middle of a building? This is, however, the main West Coast corporate headquarters for the Chiat/Day advertising agency, and the building is its giant billboard. Although not obvious from the front, the building is designed on an L-shaped plan. The binoculars lead into the main building as well as the three underground parking lots and were designed by the building's architect, Frank Gehry, in collaboration with the artists Claes Oldenburg and Coosje van Bruggen. Each eyepiece has a skylight oculus, and inside there are areas for private conferencing and research. On one side the wall is shaped like the hull of a boat and is designed to keep the western sun out, whereas the other side is made up of copper-covered rectangular columns and diagonal beams that also are designed to provide welcome shade from the burning sunshine.

UNITED EQUIPMENT COMPANY, TURLOCK, CA

RIGHT Exciting and strange buildings can be found in even the most unpromising places, as this extraordinary building in the heartland of conventional California proves. This is every big boy's dream — a building shaped like an oversized yellow Caterpillar model D6 pushing a heavy load of massive boulders! But it is not just an oversized truck; inside are the corporate offices of the United Equipment Company, admittedly not very big, but very stylish. Cunningly disguised, it contains two stories and six rooms.

BEST STORE, SACRAMENTO, CA

Now called the Notch Building, the Best Store in Sacramento, California, was originally commissioned for the retail group Best Products as one of a number of their office buildings from sculptor and architect James Wines and his SITE environmental design practice. Wines is the architect of a number of wacky but environmentally sound buildings. The founders and owners of Best Products were husband and wife serious art collectors Sidney and Francis Lewis. They wanted unconventional, innovative and thought-provoking designs for their offices in the early 1970s. The subsequent buildings produced for the company are credited as being the first stirrings of deconstructivism and the earliest reactions against the formality of modern design. Best Products in time went bankrupt, and their unique buildings struggled to find new owners. The only other extant one is the Forest Building in Richmond, now an unconventional church.

THE RASIN BUILDING, PRAGUE, CZECH REPUBLIC

RIGHT AND PAGES 124–25 Also known as "The Dancing Building" or "Ginger and Fred" (after Ginger Rogers and Fred Astaire), but officially named the Rasin Building, this extraordinary construction looks as if it is waltzing its way around the old historic heart of Prague. The building occupies a prominent position beside the River Vltava on a former World War II bomb site of a small late-19th-century neo-Renaissance building and echoes the damage inflicted by conflict on the city. The building was designed by Frank Gehry and his Czech co-architect, Vlado Milunic, in the latest deconstructive architectural style, also, for obvious reasons, called catastrophe architecture. This is inevitably a controversial structure, located as it is in historic central Prague. Construction started in 1994 and finished two years later. Its seven stories are made up of 99 different-shaped and sized concrete panels that twist and turn, bulge and sag, as if to their own musical accompaniment.

삼성증권

JONGNO TOWER, SEOUL, SOUTH KOREA

Jongno (Bell Street) in central Seoul is one of the South Korean capital's most important east-to-west thoroughfares and has long been a financial and cultural center. The Jongno Tower built there was the result of collaboration between a local firm of architects, Samoo Architects and Engineers, and Rafael Vinoly Architects. Work on the tower was completed in 1999, and it was awarded a gold award for architectural design by Seoul's metropolitan authority the following year. The 433-foot (132-meter) structure consists of 33 stories, most of which are given over to office space, although there is a restaurant with panoramic views of the city on the top floor.

NEW YORK, NEW YORK, LAS VEGAS, NV

As befits the larger-than-life center of gambling in the United States, this modern casino complex in Las Vegas takes a slice of the vibrancy and skyline of the famed Big Apple and recreates it in the Nevadan desert — albeit on a one-third scale. The complex was completed in 1997 and includes a dozen or so buildings or areas from New York, including the Brooklyn Bridge, the Empire State Building and the Statue of Liberty. Gamblers can be accommodated in more than 2,000 rooms and can play in an 84,000-square-foot (25,600-square-meter) casino. Other facilities include various restaurants, shops, a roller coaster and a substantial outdoor pool.

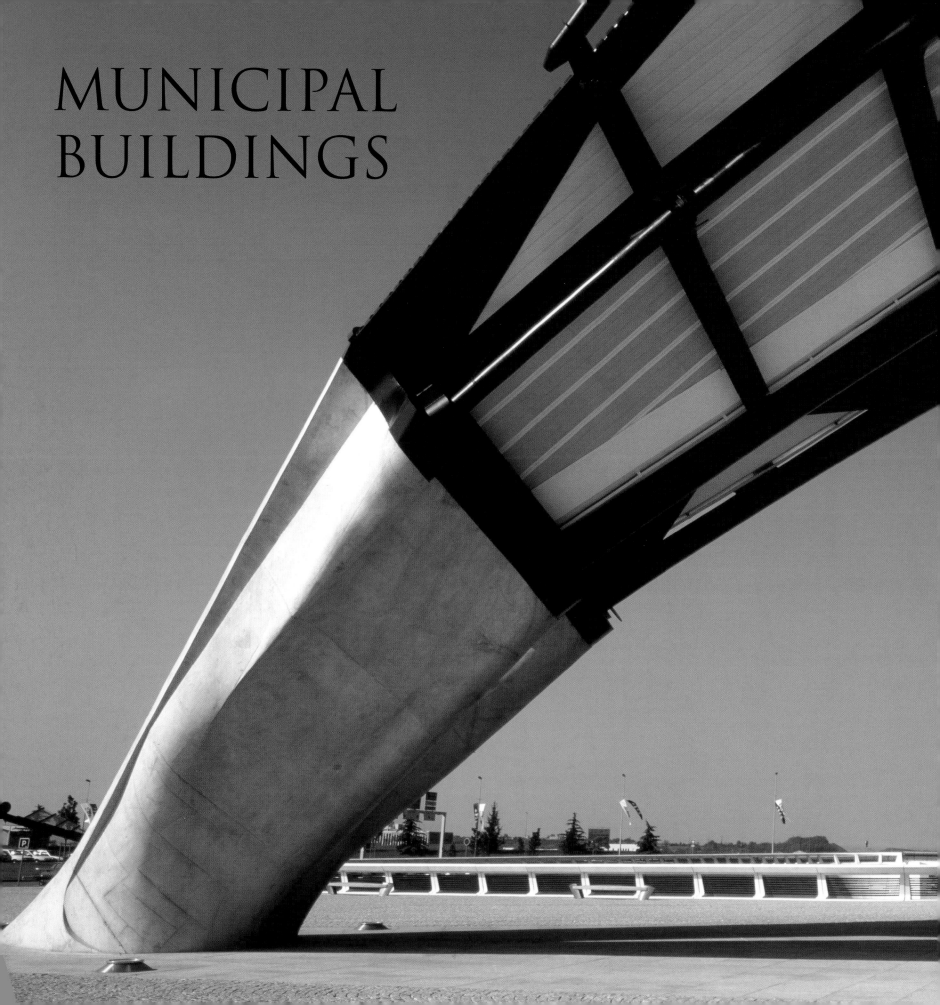

MUNICIPAL
BUILDINGS

FEDERATION SQUARE, MELBOURNE, AUSTRALIA

Chosen following a design competition and opened in October 2002 after eight controversial years of escalating costs, planning disputes and construction, Federation Square is apparently equally loved and hated by the citizens of Melbourne. It was originally intended to be complete for 2001 and the Centenary of Australian Federation, but problems, including building over the railroad lines of the former Princes Bridge railroad station without disruption, caused delays. When completed, the project, designed by Don Bates and Peter Davidson of Lab Architecture Studio, was unveiled as a public civic center and meeting place that forms a rough "U" shape surrounding a central desert ochre-colored piazza reminiscent of the outback, with surrounding buildings representing the forests. The design is composed of a pinwheel grid to "define a new sense of surface and form." The buildings around the square include a number of cafes and restaurants, as well as the Australian Centre for the Moving Image (ACMI), the Ian Potter Centre, NGV Australia, the BMW Edge auditorium, the TV headquarters for local SBS (Special Broadcasting Service) and the Melbourne Tourist Information Centre.

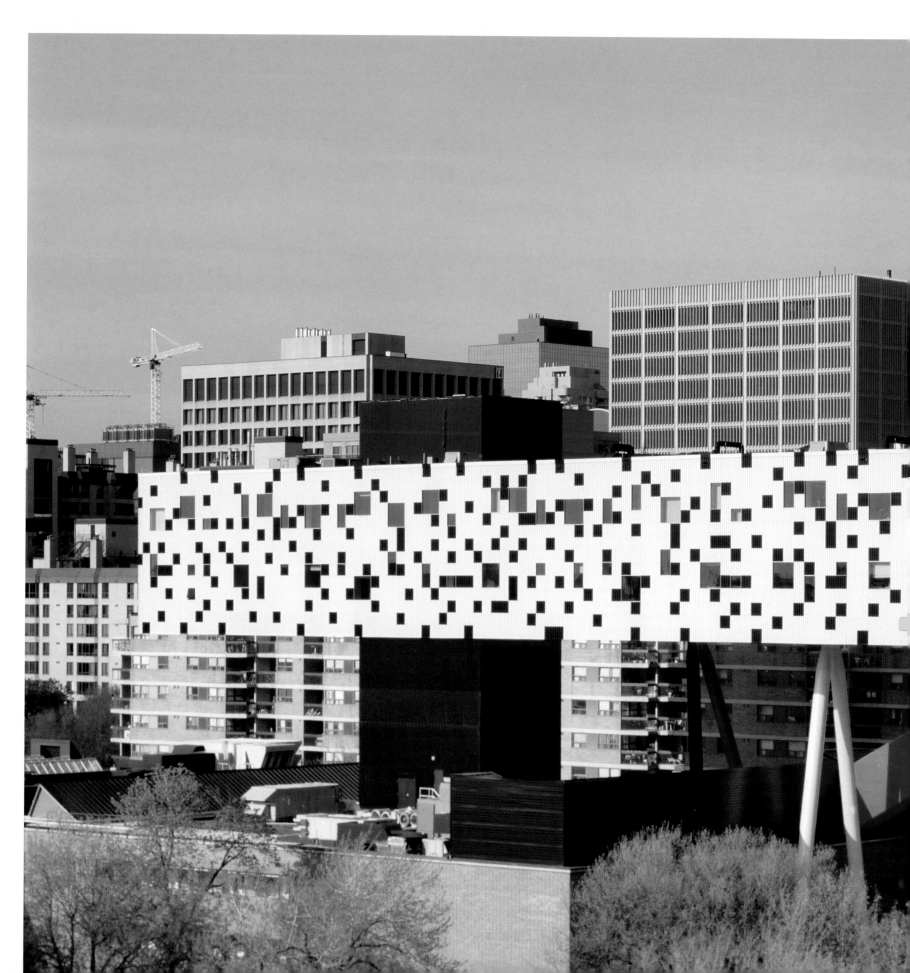

ONTARIO COLLEGE OF ART & DESIGN, TORONTO, CANADA

LEFT AND PAGES 136–37 One of the more bizarre sights in Canada is the new $42.5 million campus redevelopment and extension for the Ontario College of Art & Design (OCAD) known as the Sharp Centre for Design. Towering nine stories above the site of a former police station now stands a vast black and white "tabletop," held up by 12 differently colored and variously angled steel legs. The "tabletop" or "shoe box" contains four stories of studios and teaching space 85 feet (26 meters or 15 stories) off the ground, leaving the area underneath free for a variety of uses — such as a performance space, parking lot or any other use. This multiaward-winning venture was designed by Will Alsop, of Alsop Architects, in a joint venture with Toronto-based Robbie/Young + Wright Architects Inc. The project was completed in 2004 and has been deliberately designed so that it can be extended to the north if the need arises and the funds allocated. One suggestion from the architect is that a vast steel cage could be slung underneath the tabletop to function as a lecture hall or even as a student pub!

TOKYO CITY HALL, JAPAN

LEFT In a city with as much innovative architecture as Tokyo it takes an extraordinary building to stand out. One such building is the City Hall, which looks like something out of a science fiction movie, or as the architect, Kenzo Tange, intended, a colossal computer chip. Incredibly, construction took only three years and was completed in April 1991 in the Shinjuku district of Tokyo. The building includes three combined elements. The lowest is the parliament building, which is flanked by two rectangular towers rising in steps up to the sky. The tallest is the 48-story Tokyo Metropolitan Main building No.1 that splits into two sections — to look like a Gothic cathedral — at the 33rd level. Underground are three levels, and the top two floors are free public observation decks. Additionally, there is the eight-story Tokyo Metropolitan Assembly Building, which also has one subterranean level, and a second tower, the Tokyo Metropolitan Main Building No. 2, which has 34 stories, plus three below-ground levels. The complex was funded by public money and cost around a billion U.S. dollars — hence the local nickname Tochy, meaning "Tax Tower."

SCOTTISH PARLIAMENT BUILDING, EDINBURGH, SCOTLAND

RIGHT AND PAGES 140–43 The result of a campaign by Scotland's First Minister, Donald Dewar, for a new building to house the country's recently elected representatives, the Scottish Parliament remains a controversial structure, both economically and aesthetically. The plan is said to represent the concepts of the ancient Greek "agora," an open public meeting place where the people gathered to support the democratic ideal, and a parliament's physical union with the land that it governs. Dewar's competition was won by Spaniard Enric Mirralles, who presented the jury not with a completed scheme but with a design proposal: a handful of bent stalks and folded leaves that he proceeded to arrange on a table, creating an organic diagram of a complex that appeared to flow out of the landscape. Those leaves and stalks are everywhere, woven into the fabric of the building, from spreading skylights to sinuous steel microphone stands. They appear most graphically as the bent oak grills of the projecting window seats that cling to the facade like so many futuristic sedan chairs.

A 21st-century cathedral in terms of craft and skill, the expensive detailing is an essential part of the beautiful visual vocabulary Mirralles created to articulate the concept of a parliament embodying the land itself.

BICENTENNIAL CONSERVATORY, ADELAIDE BOTANICAL GARDENS, AUSTRALIA

PAGES 144–45 This hothouse was built in Adelaide's botanical gardens in 1988 to celebrate Australia's bicentennial. It was the work of an Australian architect, Guy Maron, who produced a curvilinear design measuring some 328 feet (100 meters) long by 154 feet (47 meters) wide by 89 feet (27 meters) high. The conservatory consists of a steel frame that supports the toughened glass comprising the doors, roof and walls. Inside there are two walkways through a controlled environment, one at ground level and the other at tree canopy height, to allow visitors to view various lowland tropical rainforest plants from north Australia, Indonesia, Papua New Guinea and various nearby Pacific Islands.

ORION BUILDING, LONDON METRO UNIVERSITY, ENGLAND

Rising unexpectedly out of the north London streets is a new Graduate Centre for the London Metropolitan University, designed by avant-garde architect, Daniel Libeskind. The building opened in March 2004 and provides improved staff and student facilities, although, arguably, its main function is to use its unusual form to draw additional visitors to the many cultural events hosted in its galleries and seminar rooms. The building comprises three intercepting elements (the three stars of Orion's belt) that combine and emphasize the connection between the university and the public. The basic concrete structure is clad with a system of triangular stainless steel panels that provide a continuously changing pattern of reflected light, enlivening the plain surfaces of the irregular block.

RAY AND MARIA STATA CENTER, CAMBRIDGE, MA

This Center for the Computer, Information, and Intelligence Sciences is part of a major expansion plan by the renowned Massachusetts Institute of Technology and is located on the northeast edge of the campus on a 2.8-acre (1.13-hectare) site. It is named after and funded by a former student and his wife and was designed by cutting-edge architect Frank Gehry. The center opened in 2004 and houses research facilities, classrooms, auditoriums and fitness and childcare facilities. The exterior, which is supported by steel and concrete, is clad in 12,800 stainless steel panels, one million bricks, painted aluminum and nearly 71,000 square feet (6,600 square meters) of glass.

COMMONWEALTH COURTS, ADELAIDE, AUSTRALIA

LEFT The Adelaide Commonwealth Law Courts are built beside the ancient meeting place of the Kuarna peoples and are designed to reflect the local culture and environment. After extensive consultation with the judiciary and court administrative staff, the law courts for South Australia received the go-ahead for this environmentally sustainable building. Deliberately making the most of local materials and vernacular architecture, the colors and shapes of the courts reflect the passing seasons. The building is clad in green patinated copper sheeting and the interiors feature locally quarried granites and sandstones with wooden fittings made from the indigenous Red River gum tree. All of the 22 courtrooms have natural light and external views, which are deliberately designed to evoke concentration and calm through what can be difficult legal processes. The western interior is bathed in natural light brought in through an 88-foot-high (26.8-meter-high) sculptural space that rises up through the five floors of the building, connecting the various levels with public walkways and meeting areas.

WATERPUMP GEMAAL, AMSTERDAM, THE NETHERLANDS

RIGHT The Netherlands is largely a country dominated by water, both sea and fresh. Three major rivers — the Rhine, Maas and Scheldt — reach the North Sea through the low-lying country, and much of its present area, around 40 percent, has been recovered from the sea. The authorities face a continuous battle to protect the country from flooding and have created an extensive network of embankments, canals, barriers and pumping stations to keep water out and remove excess from the water table. As this elegant water pumping station near the capital, Amsterdam, shows, industrial architecture does not have to be purely functional but can also be pleasing to the eye.

TGV STATION, LYON, FRANCE

LEFT, RIGHT AND PAGES 154–55 Head down, metallic wings swept back, the ticket hall of Lyon-Satolas Airport is a predatory bird whose concrete beak plunges into the ground, directly into the path of oncoming passengers with their luggage-laden trolleys. With such obvious connotations of flight, it comes as something of a surprise to find that its architect, Santiago Calatrava, claims his primary inspiration to have been the human eye rather than the hovering hawk. Glancing to either side of the cathedral-like ticket hall interior, the delicate steel glazing bars do indeed appear like long eyelashes sprouting from the low-arching concrete "lids" to reach the swooping curve of the ceiling that reaches 131 feet (40 meters) into the air. From here the passengers turn left or right to descend, via banks of escalators, onto sunken platforms, where they are treated to further displays of sculptural fineness. The platform canopies extend out like racks of bleached prehistoric ribs, their faceted and polished concrete members supporting glazed sections between their fingers, flooding the concourse with natural light. Such synthesis of art and architecture has made Calatrava one of the world's most iconic architects, whose prolific output of photogenic "creatures" is rivaled only by Frank Gehry.

BUS STATION HOOFDDORP, THE NETHERLANDS

LEFT, RIGHT AND PAGES 158–59 Polystyrene may seen like an unpromising material for architecture, but avant-garde architects NIO Architecten have successfully employed the ubiquitous white foam to create the largest building in the world, made entirely from synthetic materials. Wrapped around itself like a snoozing boa constrictor, the Spaarne Hospital Bus Station looks like it might contemplate swallowing the green and blue buses that nervously circle its concrete plinth. The architects themselves call it the "Amazing Whale Jaw," imagining it to be the beached remains of a vast ocean-going mammal. An impressive 164 feet (50 meters) in length, the whole building was made off-site in workshops using computer-controlled cutting machines, and then delivered in five sections to be glued together and sprayed with a final coat of polyester. The lightweight sections were easy for workmen to maneuver into position, but they wasted no time in bolting the snake to the ground as it would have slithered away in a strong breeze. All the necessary functions have been accommodated within the form, including litter bins, bench seats, recesses for lighting and even a restroom for the bus drivers to sit, quietly drinking tea in heavily insulated comfort.

TWA TERMINAL, NEW YORK, NY

LEFT AND RIGHT Given that mass aviation has become a daily reality for countless millions, it is hard to imagine how impossibly glamorous the concept of transcontinental air travel appeared to the first generation of jet-setters. Back in the late 1950s, instead of a mind-numbing assault course of security check-ins and baggage carousels, passengers enjoyed a level of exclusivity and service that made boarding the early jet-airliners akin to catching the Orient Express. TWA recognized that their point of departure demanded this sense of occasion and commissioned architect Eero Saarinen to create a distinctive transport hub that could be used as a concrete form of corporate identity. Saarinen's response came closer to capturing the essence of flight than any building before or since, a consummate demonstration of his unique synthesis of art and engineering. Four leaping concrete shells, their cantilevered peaks echoing the tail fins and wing tips of the planes they served, converge upon a central hall some 50 feet (15 meters) high and 315 feet (96 meters) long. The rough boards used as shuttering leave a richly textured surface, a warm, hand-made finish that catches the light. Gazing through the full-height glazing, waiting passengers find themselves with ringside seats to watch the silver planes performing the miracle of flight.

CULTURAL BUILDINGS

SYDNEY OPERA HOUSE, AUSTRALIA

Jørn Utzon's expressive masterpiece has come to define the world's image of Sydney, but there were moments when the fabled opera house looked as though it would simply fail to rise above the harbor's waves. Utzon won the 1957 competition largely thanks to the late intervention of juror Eero Saarinen, who arrived after the judging panel had already made the first edit of the 234 entries. He famously rescued Utzon's submission from the rejected pile, announcing, "Gentlemen, this is the first prize." Saarinen recommended the services of talented British engineer Ove Arup, but both he and Utzon struggled to find a mathematical fingerhold with which to get to grips with the seductive freehand curving forms of the winning sketches. It was only after work had begun on site that Utzon had his eureka moment and devised a way of generating the essential engineering data by changing all the shells to correlate to fragments of an imaginary sphere, some 300 feet (91.4 meters) in diameter. With this breakthrough the shells could be redesigned using a common system of precast concrete ribs covered with tapered panels clad in over a million glazed Swedish tiles, giving rise to the muscular ceramic sails that made the building a 20th-century icon.

CASA DA MUSICA, PORTO, PORTUGAL

The majority of the world's opera houses are stately stone neo-classical palaces, but not so Rem Koolhaas' Casa Da Musica, which rears up like some irregular boulder brought from the quarries that supplied the materials for its predecessors. The dramatically leaning concrete faces, some tilted at a dizzying 60 degrees, are mutually dependent. The scaffolding that surrounded them during construction could not be removed until the roof slab had been cast in place, anchoring the walls into permanent equilibrium. It is not only the exterior that breaks operatic conventions as the main auditorium is opened to the outside world at both front and back, bringing daylight flooding into what is normally a hermetically sealed environment. Instead of exotic veneers and gilded cherubs Koolhaas lined this tunnel-like interior with simple plywood panels and then wryly chose to magnify the wood's grain to create the overlaid pattern applied in gold leaf. The curious suspended frame that hovers above the stage is covered in a stretched PVC fabric that can be inflated or deflated, altering the acoustics to suit the type of music being played below. The building may not be in tune with conservative tastes, but it can at least be relied upon to resonate with the performers.

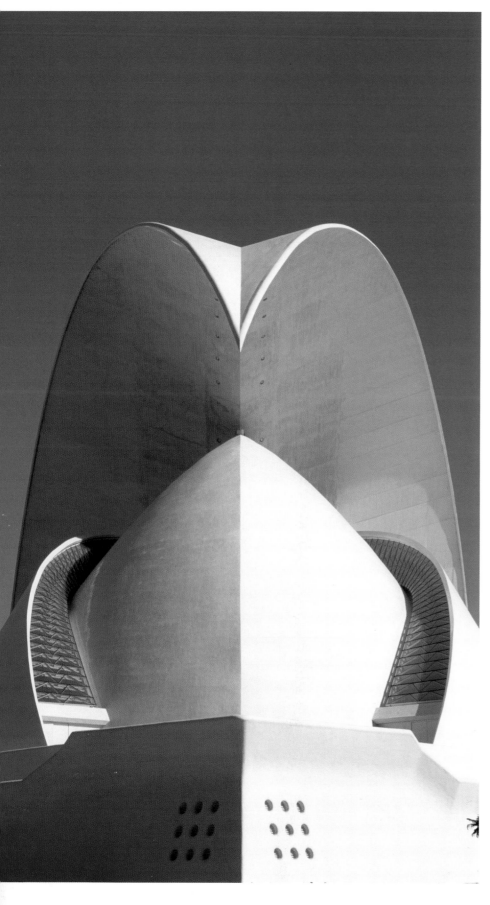

AUDITORIO DE TENERIFE, SANTA CRUZ, SPAIN

A wave of culture has broken upon the shores of Tenerife, a destination normally associated with beaches of sunburned British tourists, sleeping off a night of sangria-fueled excitement. But now the famous holiday resort can offer a more cultural form of relaxation in the form of a 21st-century concert hall that has all the swagger of a baroque cathedral. The Auditorio de Tenerife is built in a prime location on reclaimed land overlooking the harbor of Santa Cruz. The concrete cone-shaped auditorium seems to make a passing reference to the island's volcanic past, its summit grazing the underside of the leaping wave-like canopy that looks poised to engulf it. Inside it contains a 1,600-seater symphonic hall, while a smaller 428-seat chamber music hall lies further back in its tail. The distinctive canopy, curving like a seagull's beak or a foaming bow wave, rises to nearly 197 feet (60 meters) at its peak, acting as a marker that can be seen for miles around. The hall's curvaceous exterior is clad in a mosaic of broken white-glazed ceramic tiles called "trencadis," a finish that harks back to the art nouveau creations of Antoni Gaudi that have long inspired Calatrava's work.

KUNSTHAUS GRAZ, AUSTRIA

LEFT, BELOW AND PAGES 172–73 As it began its tenure as "European City of Culture," the quiet town of Graz received an exuberant guest, a "friendly alien," as residents called it, which had come to stay. With its dark, irregular, undulating form bulging out to fill the spaces in between the red-tiled roofs, the Kunsthaus immediately stood out against the town's orderly pastel-toned architecture. The building's outer skin is cloaked in 6½ x 10 feet (2 x 3 meter) acrylic panels that sandwich 925 circular light fittings against the inner wall. These form "BIX" (big pixels), which are controlled by computer to transform the skin into a media facade, a rippling mass of pulsing patterns, images and text that beams messages across the city at night. The architects modeled the skin using software designed for the shipping industry, and the organic curves seem to display a sense of hydrodynamics, as though it has been shaped by water. Its back is studded with 16 angled nozzles that stretch out like a nest of hungry chicks impatiently waiting for their evening meal. The interior galleries are partially lit by the nozzles' skylights, backed up by concentric rings of fluorescent tubes, giving them the appearance of teleportation devices ready to abduct the unwary visitor.

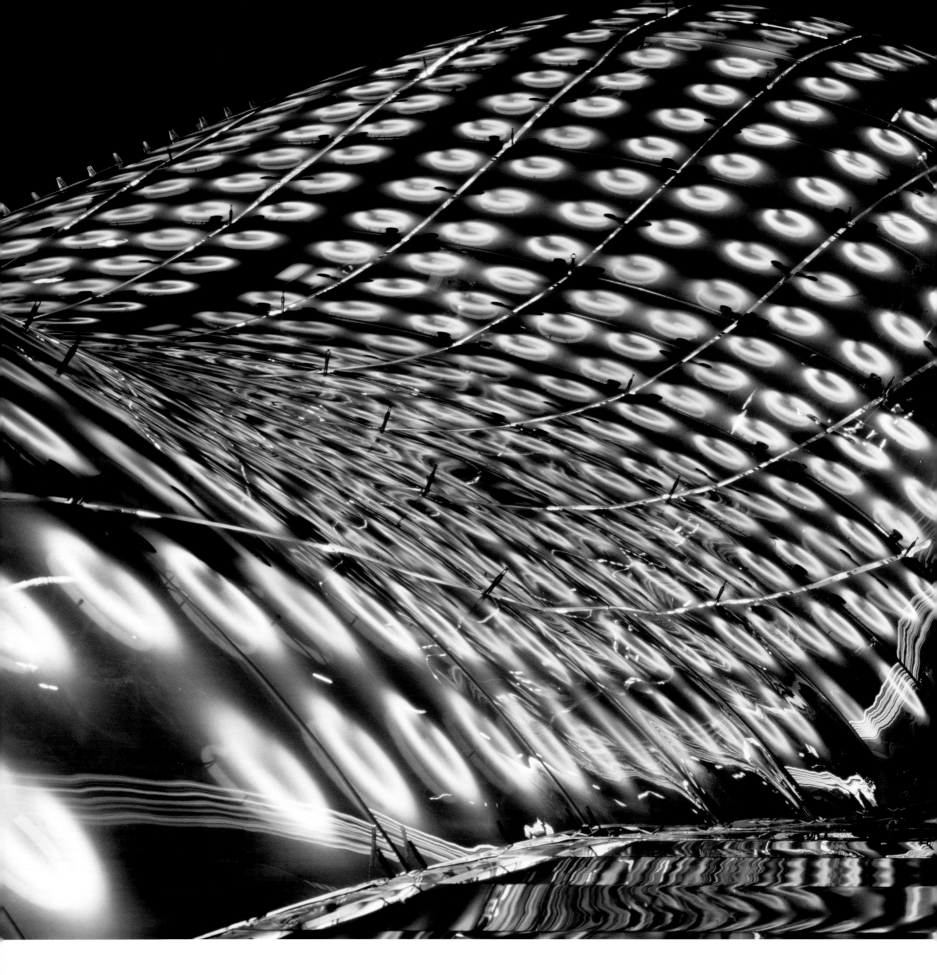

MEDIA STAND, LORDS CRICKET GROUND, LONDON, ENGLAND

The Marylebone Cricket Club is an unlikely patron for avant-garde architecture, but something about Future System's design for the media center at Lords Cricket Ground must have caught their imagination for there it hovers between the Compton and Edrich grandstands, the flying saucer of the sporting world. Poised as if preparing to land on the batsman's crease, the Natwest Media Centre can play host to up to 200 journalists and commentators, providing them with an unrivaled view of play from its banked tiers of seats. Conscious that the act of observation should not conflict with the interests of the game, the architects tilted the laminated glass screen at 25 degrees, ensuring that the sun's reflections do not blind the players. The world's first entirely aluminum building, the stand's smooth, aerodynamic skin hides a wealth of welded struts and beams employing a fabrication technique borrowed from the hulls of speed boats and racing yachts. The whole structure was actually built in a Dutch boatyard and shipped to England in 9.8 feet (3 meter) wide sections to be welded into position on site. Expensive connotations of hand-built motor launches must have sat well with the client, making such a futuristic building palatable to a normally conservative institution.

SINGAPORE PERFORMING ARTS CENTRE, SINGAPORE

The Esplanade or Singapore Performing Arts Centre sits on the shore of Marina Bay, beside the Singapore River, between the old city on one side and the business and entertainment district on the other. The design is a careful combination of harmony with nature and a balance of yin and yang. Its unusual prickly double domes have earned it the nickname of "Durians" in reference to its likeness to the "king of fruits," the delicious but smelly durian, a great local favorite. Less flattering allusions compare it to two frisky aardvarks, microphones or a pair of Chinese dumplings. But these remarkable spiky, translucent roofs are not just for show; they change pattern according to the sun and control the internal environment of the pavilions. The center was designed and built to be the biggest performing arts center and exhibition space in Singapore, where a variety of arts can flourish. The complex contains five auditoriums and several outdoor performance spaces plus a mix of offices, stores and apartments. Completed in 2002, it has become one of Singapore's architectural landmarks.

ALLIANZ ARENA, MUNICH, GERMANY

The newest and most expensive of the 12 World Cup stadia used in 2006 at a cost of 280 million euros, the Allianz Arena in Munich opened its doors for the first time on May 30, 2005 for a game between TSV 1860 Munich and FC Nuremberg, followed the day after by the arena's other tenants, FC Bayern Munich, taking on the German national team. The brand new stadium was designed by celebrity Swiss architects Jacques Herzog and Pierre de Meuron after plans to renovate Munich's old ground, the Olympiastadion, were rejected. Whatever they came up with had a monumental act to follow — the Olympiastadion was once the best stadium in West Germany and then the whole of Germany, with its innovative tent-like roof design. The new stadium is their idea of a futuristic football stadium, its one of a kind bubble-like design made up of no less than 2,874 inflatable foil cushions that are UV-permeable and unaffected by any weather conditions. These cushions act as a projection surface to bathe the stadium in either red or blue, depending on which of its tenants are playing at the time — Bayern Munich or TSV 1860 Munich. Although insurance company Allianz holds the naming rights to the stadium until 2021, the tenants have let it be known the term alliance also represents the friendship between the two clubs. The impressive Allianz Arena — ground capacity 66,000 — had the honor of staging the 2006 tournament's opening fixture, followed by three more group games, a knockout game and the semifinal.

MUSEU DE ARTE CONTEMPORÂNEA (MAC), NITERÓI, RIO DE JANEIRO, BRAZIL

Perched upon a rocky peninsula overlooking Guanabara Bay, the Museu De Arte Contemporânea floats like an architectural throwback to the Dan Dare Eagle comics of the 1950s, with its UFO exterior and spiraling red boarding ramp. But architect Oscar Niemeyer has a surprisingly organic interpretation of his white machined form, thinking of it as a budding flower, rising on its single stem from the nourishing pool of water at its base. The elegant form does indeed bear a marked resemblance to another florally inspired design, the iconic fiberglass Tulip chair by Eero Saarrinen, albeit on a much grander scale. With a "stem" some 30 feet (9 meters) thick, rising 52 feet (16 meters) high, the reinforced concrete flower holds a three-level gallery that displays João Sattamini's personal collection of Brazilian contemporary art, the loan of which was conditional upon Niemeyer creating a fitting home in which it could be hung. The small footprint of the single-column form allowed the architect to push the 164 feet (50 meter) wide gallery to the very edge of the narrow site, improving the spectacular views from the 360-degree black-tinted windows and endowing the museum with the dual function of educational art house and sensational observation platform.

MUSEUM OF CIVILIZATION, GATINEAU, CANADA

What do you get these days for $213 million? The answer is this vast and astonishing museum in the city of Gatineau, Quebec, built in a unique style, dubbed "New Age Native American." The Museum of Civilization arrived a year late and wildly over budget but, nevertheless, to great critical acclaim. When construction started in 1983 the budget was $78 million and the plans were far from complete — the only agreed on criterion was that this was a museum designed to celebrate Native Americans, their culture and environment. The architect, Douglas Cardinal, likens his museum — over which he battled the accountants, bureaucrats and anyone else with an opinion — to having been sculpted by a glacier with outcroppings and irregular topographical shapes, meandering pathways and stunning vistas. Made out of limestone that has been cut into dramatic curves and ellipses, with granite floors and copper roofs, the building has been called the most eccentric museum in the world. Some of the many wonders in addition to its three-and-a-half-million artifact collection include an artificial stream that cascades in a waterfall beside the grand staircase and across part of the central plaza, life-sized Indian camps and entire replicas of 500-year-old townscapes.

CENTRE POMPIDOU, PARIS, FRANCE

LEFT, RIGHT AND PAGES 186–87 Not since the Eiffel Tower rose into the sky in 1889 has a building caused so much Parisian consternation as the Centre Pompidou. Selected from 681 entries, Richard Rogers' and Renzo Pianos' winning design brazenly turned its back on the traditional galleries of old, turning itself inside out in the process. The concept was surprisingly simple, even though the engineering was suitably high-tech. To gain the maximum column-free interior floor space, the architects banished all the building's services to the exterior. A riot of color, the facades bulge with red, green and blue pipes and ducts, all contained within the grid of 13 cross-braced white girder bays that fill the full width of the site. So great was the space saving that the building did not fill the whole plot, allowing the creation of the Beaubourg Plaza, which rapidly became a focal point for tourists and entertainers, creating a vibrant center for street culture that matched the buzz of the art exhibits. The most memorable feature is the theatrical glazed escalator tube that snakes up five stories to reach the roof terrace café, providing visitors with easy access to every level while presenting a constantly unfolding spectacle of the capital.

JEWISH MUSEUM, BERLIN, GERMANY

Two thousand years of Jewish culture in Germany are celebrated in Daniel Libeskind's Jewish Museum in Berlin, but as part of atonement for the Holocaust, many critics wanted the building to remain pristine and empty of artifacts. The building itself is as important as any of the exhibits; it is clad in cold zinc and the entrance to the museum is via a subterranean passageway. Everything is deliberately designed to be disorienting and disturbing, to promote feelings of insecurity, claustrophobia and panic. The outside world is only occasionally glimpsed through window slits, and the shapes of the rooms distort sounds. Everything deliberately makes the visitor uncomfortable and disturbed. Perhaps the most unsettling area is the Holocaust Tower, where a massive door thunders shut behind the visitor and the only light and sound come from a tiny shaft high up the wall. Outside the main building is the Garden of Exile, with a tilting pathway flanked with oddly angled pillars. Once through this part of the building, the museum becomes much more comfortable and conventional.

STAATSGALERIE STUTTGART, GERMANY

It seems fitting that a British architect was given the opportunity to make good the damage wrought by Allied bombers in World War II, by winning the competition to build an extension to the Stuttgart's 19th-century Staatsgalerie, (the state gallery). Concerned with preserving the remaining fabric of the city, James Stirling's design retained elements of the partly ruined museum, incorporating them into a series of stepped terraces built into the steep hillside site. The design combines many of the hard geometric forms normally associated with cold, white modernist buildings, but here they are transformed into warm, monumental strata of heavily veined sandstone and travertine. The austerity of the plain stonework is offset by the bright blue, red and green oversized metal handrails that edge the building's curves, like lines of pigment squeezed directly from a tube of artist's color. Walking by the entrance wall, visitors encounter one of Stirling's little architectural joke: a series of masonry blocks appear to have fallen out of the facade, as though Indiana Jones has effected an escape from a crypt-like basement. In fact, this is a purpose-built opening to the ventilation ducts for the subterranean parking garages, deliberately located under the building to free up space for open public plazas above.

PHAENO SCIENCE CENTER, WOLFSBURG, GERMANY

Cruising at low altitude over the town of Wolfsburg, the concrete prow of Zaha Hadid's Phaeno Science Center points purposefully into the square like an angular Star-Destroyer. Its unworldly appearance is enhanced by the undulating ramps and curves of the surrounding lunar landscape that visitors must negotiate before boarding the craft. The center floats 23 feet (7 meters) above street level on 10 inverted concrete cones that rise up out of this park of dunes and craters. By elevating the building on its 10 irregular feet, like concrete vortexes sucked down from floor above, Hadid created a second public realm beneath the vessel's hull, eerily illuminated by dozens of fluorescent tubes hidden in square recesses. Carved into one of the cones, the coffee bar's blue glow helps further illuminate the cavernous undercroft, like a teleporter waiting to whisk visitors to the wonders of the galleries above. All this freeform, fluid structure was made possible only by the largest single use of self-compacting concrete ever attempted in Europe. By including a superplasticizing additive into the mix, the concrete was made to flow freely into the complex shuttering, without the need for thorough vibration, which would have been an impossible task given the intricacies of the futuristic mold.

TJIBAOU CULTURAL CENTRE, NOUMEA, NEW CALEDONIA

Exactly 20 years after his competition-winning Centre Pompidou, revered architect Renzo Piano found himself designing a building to immortalize the name of a prominent adversary of French rule instead of its figurehead. Piano had won the contest to create a cultural center in memory of Jean Marie Tjibaou, a leading figure in the campaign for recognition of the Kanak culture, a Polynesian way of life that had almost been extinguished by French colonial policies. Taking his inspiration from the indigenous forms of the Kanak's "Great Houses," Piano fashioned a series of open-sided towers whose clusters of crisply cut fingers emulate the halfway stage in the centuries-old Kanak technique of raising their conical palm sapling hut roofs. Instead of binding their ends together to form the usual peak, Piano left them pointing to the sky, symbolizing the continued growth of a culture brought back from the edge of oblivion. The beautifully detailed towers, with their laminated iroko ribs and stainless steel ties, help to ventilate the adjoining low-lying structures, the prevailing breeze passing over their slanting roofs creating currents that draw fresh air through the interior.

A sculptural blend of tradition and modernity, Piano's solution is a worthy monument to Tjibaou's legacy.

EDEN PROJECT, BODELVA, ST. AUSTELL, CORNWALL, ENGLAND

Bubbling out of the depths of a Cornish china clay pit, the Eden project is the 21st-century heir to the geodesic domes of Buckminster Fuller. The largest conservatory in the world, its interlocking forms are divided to create two climactic zones or "biomes," one devoted to the humid tropics and the other to warm and temperate regions. Built on an unprecedented scale, the Humid Biome is some 287 feet (240 meters) long and 361 feet (110 meters) wide, its curving apex reaching 180 feet (55 meters) into the air. The hexagonal modules that form the basic building blocks vary in size, with the largest being 36 feet (11 meters) across. The biomes' floral inhabitants are quite literally cushioned against the inclement British weather by pneumatic pillows of ETFE (ethylene tetrafluoroethylene) zipped into the hexagonal frames. This space-age polymer was the key to Nicholas Grimshaw's elegant architectural solution, as pumping air between three layers of ETFE creates a sandwich with the same insulation properties as double-glazing, but with only 1% of the dead weight of glass. ETFE's self-cleaning antistatic surface, 40-year life span and final biodegradability all add up to that rare thing: a plastic with green credentials.

GUGGENHEIM MUSEUM BILBAO, SPAIN

LEFT, RIGHT AND PAGES 200–201 Built in Spain's Basque Country alongside the Nervion River, the Guggenheim Museum Bilbao was designed by Canadian-American architect Frank Gehry to house a collection of both permanent and visiting exhibits featuring works of Spanish and international artists. A huge tourist attraction, drawing visitors from around the globe, Gehry's design is radical, a brilliant example of the style of architecture called "deconstructivism." This style sprang from postmodern architecture in the late 1980s and is characterized by non-linear processes of design and nonrectilinear shapes. Opened in 1997, the museum is one of five major international museums (the others are in New York, Venice, Berlin and Las Vegas) constructed under the aegis of the Solomon R. Guggenheim Foundation. A sixth, in Abu Dhabi, also designed by Gehry, should open in 2011. The photographs on this spread and the following show this extraordinary building and give a feel for its impact by day and night.

EXPERIENCE MUSIC PROJECT, SEATTLE, WA

This beautifully sinuous building in Seattle, Washington, was the idea of computer software billionaire Paul G. Allen, an avid fan of Jimi Hendrix. The former turned to the Canadian-born, California-based architect Frank Gehry to turn his dream of a popular music center into reality. Gehry stated that he gained inspiration for the design from a pile of rubbish he collected from an electric guitar store in Santa Monica. Construction work took place during 1999 and 2000 using a fabricated steel frame clad with shotcrete and sheet metal panels. The center contains, among other facilities, recording studios, performance spaces and a museum with 80,000 artifacts.

THE SAGE, GATESHEAD, ENGLAND

Partly inspired by the leaping arches of the neighboring Tyne-side bridges, the Sage appears like a cascading wall of water about to flood the river's banks. The pixelated exterior, engineered by Buro Happold, covers a single span of 262 feet (80 meters) and supports 3,000 linen-finish stainless steel cladding panels that catch the changing light of the equally steely northern skies. A further 280 glass panes provide the Sage with glowing "eyes" that furnish waiting audiences with views out over the Tyne. Together with Wilkinson Eyre's Millennium Bridge and the converted Baltic Four Mill art gallery, the Sage forms part of a trio of projects intended to regenerate the former industrial center, and has been deliberately designed to be as inclusive and welcoming as possible. Foster & Partners created the arching canopy's three ridges to act as "shrink wrapping" for three separate auditoriums that offer a wide spectrum of musical and cultural events. Unifying these performance spaces with cafés and bars under one roof creates an informal social hub where both artists and their audiences rub shoulders, protected from the elements.

THE IMPERIAL WAR MUSEUM NORTH, SALFORD QUAYS, ENGLAND

This museum lies in the rejuvenated Salford Quays area of the city of Manchester in northern England and was designed by Daniel Libeskind, the Polish-born but naturalized U.S. architect. His design strives to depict a world torn into three parts by conflict with each part representing war either on land, at sea or in the air. Work commenced on the aluminum-clad waterside building in August 1998 and the structure was completed in June 2000. The interior contains exhibition spaces, rooms for conferences and private functions, a café and restaurant, academic study facilities and a shop. The award-winning museum opened its doors to the public in 2002.

THE LOUVRE, PARIS, FRANCE

French President Francois Mitterand initiated a major program to upgrade the world-renowned Louvre Museum in Paris during 1981. The Chinese-American architect Leoh Ming Pei was asked to create a new entrance to the complex in its central Napoleon's Courtyard and he devised a transparent pyramid with four sides of 115 feet (35 meters) and a height of about 70 feet (21 meters). It has a steel frame and the covering consists of 603 rhombus-shaped and 70 triangular-shaped plates of glass. The pyramid opened in 1989, the bicentennial of the French Revolution, and it leads to a two-level complex of shops, cafés, exhibition spaces and a reception area.

CHAPEL OF THE HOLY CROSS, SEDONA, AZ

Hanging between the clear blue sky and dramatic red rocks of Sedona, the Chapel of the Holy Cross is every bit as much a sculpture as a place of worship. Built directly into a butte 200 feet (61 meters) above the valley below, over 25,000 tons of rock had to be removed from this challenging (to say the least) site and the vast cross frontage can be seen for miles around. The chapel was the inspiration and life's ambition of sculptress, painter, philanthropist, and devout Catholic, Marguerite Brunswig Staude who was initially inspired to design and build a chapel by a personal vision of a gigantic cross superimposed over the newly built Empire State Building in 1932. Years later after an abortive attempt — with the support of Frank Lloyd Wright — to build her vision in Hungary above the River Danube in the early 1940s she decided on the red rocks of Sedona for her inspiring work. Staude strongly felt that the arts should celebrate and serve the spirit, and it was her mother's dying wish that she should see the work realized. Finally completed in 1956 the Chapel was among the first contemporary structures built by the Catholic Church and received the American Institute of Architects "The Award of Honor" in 1957.

BETH SHOLOM SYNAGOGUE, ELKINS PARK, PA

Not an obvious place of worship at first sight, the Beth Shalom Synagogue is the work of Frank Lloyd Wright, who modestly described it as a "luminous Mount Sinai." Wright died a few months before its completion in September 1959 so he never saw it in its full glory. Much of the walling and roof was made of translucent layers of wire glass (now plastic), which allows natural light to flood in during the day and glows with artificial light in the dark — resembling Mount Sinai, which according to the Bible, shone with light during the Revelation. The architect was well into his 80s when he set to work on the synagogue, and he took great care to incorporate as many Jewish symbols and elements into the infrastructure as possible. The outside is hexagonal and has been likened to two hands at worship, with the lateral extensions at the front corresponding to thumbs. Alternatively, the synagogue can be seen as reminiscent of an ancient tent tabernacle as used by the Children of Israel while they wandered for 40 years in the desert.

ANNUNCIATION GREEK ORTHODOX CHURCH, MILWAUKEE, WI

Looking rather like a decorative flying saucer, the Annunciation Greek Orthodox Church in Milwaukee was Frank Lloyd Wright's last major commission and was completed in 1961. The design of the church is based on the Greek cross — an equilateral cross within a circle — and the motif repeatedly appears throughout the church, including across the gold anodized aluminum icon screen and the gates to the exterior sunken garden. The pews and altar are in the shape of a cross, with the circular dome superimposed over the top to complete the motif. Small circular windows are strung like beads around the rim of the concrete shell dome which, to withstand the dramatic extremes of expansion and compression caused by the weather, is supported on thousands of ball bearings sitting in steel rails under the dome. Frank Lloyd Wright died before the ground was even broken on the project.

CHURCH OF THE HOLY TRINITY, GENEVA, SWITZERLAND

The past century has seen a rapid departure from previously accepted forms of ecclesiastical architecture with the church becoming as much a vehicle for avant-garde experimentation as the museum or the gallery. One of the most original was designed by Ugo Brunoni and takes the form of a stone sphere surrounded by a shallow moat, like an immense coronation orb floating in a pool of anointing oil. Clad in carefully cut masonry blocks it has a solidity and permanence to match its Gothic predecessors. Set into the church's upper hemisphere, a discrete ring of twelve circular skylights produces an internal halo of colored dots representing the apostles. An even more iconic effect is caused by the cluster of four turrets topped by cubic skylights that project four corresponding squares of sunlight down onto the high altar, the shadow lines left in between forming the sign of the cross. Like an abstract camera obscura, the church uses natural light to illuminate the story of the gospels, a truly modern interpretation of a house of God.

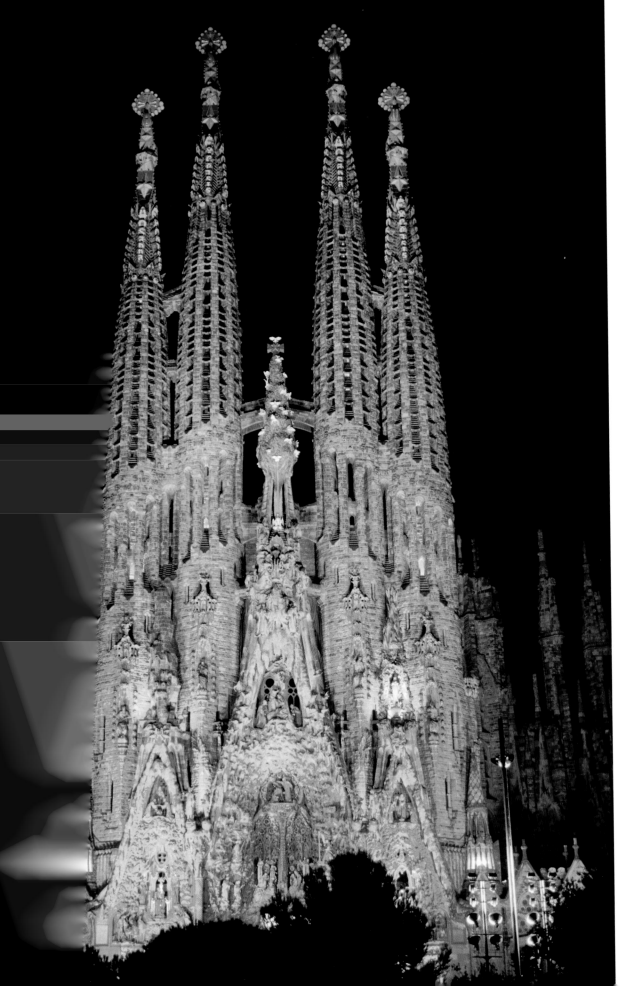

SAGRADA FAMILIA, BARCELONA, CATALONIA, SPAIN

This church in Barcelona, Catalonia, was to have been the crowning achievement of the Spanish architect Antonio Gaudi, who specialized in a style largely unique to him known as Catalan Modernism, itself a branch of the Art Nouveau movement. Gaudi was inspired by the traditional architecture of the peninsula, chiefly a blend of medieval and Arabic. The church was actually begun in the Gothic style in 1882 and Gaudi did not become involved until two years later but thereafter he worked on it until he died in 1926. The building, which is still under construction, has many traditional features of ecclesiastical architecture that have been rendered in a wholly novel way.

HALLGRIMSKIRKJA, REYKJAVIK, ICELAND

LEFT This Lutheran cathedral is situated in Reykjavik, Iceland, the most northerly capital in the world, and was designed by a state architect Gudjon Samuelson who was given the job in 1937. The building was somewhat controversial, not least because it remains the longest ever construction project in Icelandic history, lasting until the 1980s. The cathedral, the largest in the country, is named after Reverend Hallgrimur Petursson, a much loved 17th-century national poet, and lies on a hill, Skolavorduholt, that overlooks the capital's old center. Its steeple rises to a height of around 240 feet (73 meters) and the interior can accommodate up to 1,200 worshippers.

GANDHI MATAPAN, KANYAKUMARI, TAMIL NADU, INDIA

LEFT This memorial to the leading figure in India's independence movement is situated close to the town of Kanyakumari, which is in the state of Tamil Nadu, and lies at the southernmost tip of the subcontinent. It was completed in 1956, eight years after Mahatma Gandhi was assassinated, and was designed as a modern take on the traditional Hindu temples that are found in central India. The complex was built on the spot where the urn containing Gandhi's ashes was kept for public viewing and mourning before the remains were scattered in the sea. At noon every October 2, the Mahatma's birthday, the sun's rays fall on the exact spot where the urn once stood.

THE GRAND MOSQUE, DJENNE, MALI

This mosque, located in the Malian town of Djenne, is the largest structure in the world to be built out of adobe and thanks to its three imposing minarets is easily recognizable. It consists of mud bricks held together by mud mortar and covered in mud plaster to give it a smooth appearance. Planks of palm wood were inserted to hold scaffolding during construction and to give the whole complex greater stability and strength when completed. Although appearing to be quite an old structure, the mosque was in fact built between 1906 and 1909 by a workforce under the guidance of Ismaila Traore, the head of the local masons' guild.

BIBLIOGRAPHY & WEBSITES

BIBLIOGRAPHY

If this book has whet your appetite for architecture then the following recommended titles should offer plenty of food for thought.

Able, Chris: *Sky High – Vertical Architecture*; Royal Academy Publications/Thames & Hudson, London, England, 2003.

Cattermole, Paul: *Buildings For Tomorrow; Architecture That Changed Our World*; Thames & Hudson, London, England, 2006.

Curtis, William J.R. : *Modern Architecture Since 1900*; Phaidon Press Ltd., London, England 1982; Third Edition, 1996.

Dal Co, Francesco, and Forster, Kurt W. : *Frank O. Gehry – The Complete Works*; The Monacelli Press, New York, USA, 1998.

Gill, John: *Essential Gaudi*; Parragon, Bath, England, 2001.

Glancey, Jonathan: *C20th Architecture – The Structures That Shaped The Century*; Carlton Books, London, England, 1998.

Headley, Gwyn, and Meulenkamp, Wim: *Follies, Grottos & Garden Buildings*; Aurum Press, London, England 1999.

Hess, Alan: *Hyperwest – American Residential Architecture on the Edge*; Thames & Hudson, London, England, 1996.

Hess, Alan: *The Architecture of John Lautner*; Thames & Hudson, London, England, 1999.

Keiding, Martin, Dirckinck-Holmfled, Kim, and Norberg-Schulz, Christian: *Utzon And The New Tradition*; The Danish Architectural Press, Copenhagen, Denmark, 2005.

Lyall, Sutherland: *Masters of Structure – Engineering Today's Innovative Buildings*; Laurence King, London, England, 2002.

McCarter, Robert: *Frank Lloyd Wright*; Phaidon Press Ltd., London, England, 1997.

O'Neill, Paul Daniel: *Lutyens Country Houses*; The Whitney Library of Design, New York, USA, 1981.

Powell, Kenneth: *New Architecture in Britain*; Merrell Publishers Ltd., London, England, 2003.

Powell, Kenneth: *Richard Rogers – Complete Works – Volume One*; Phaidon Press Ltd., London, England, 1999.

Slessor, Catherine: *Eco-Tech – Sustainable Architecture and High Technology*; Thames & Hudson, London, England, 1997.

Various, Edited by Sabine Thiel-Siling: *Icons of Architecture – The 20th Century*; Prestel, London, England, 1998.

Various: *The Phaidon Atlas of Contemporary World Architecture*; Phaidon, London, England, 2004.

Wells, Matthew: *Skyscapers – Structures and Design*; Yale University Press, New Haven, USA, 2005.

Melvin, Jeremy: *Isms – Understanding Architecture*; Herbert Press, London, England, 2005.

WEBSITES

Other sources are architects' websites, where you can explore both past projects and work in progress. The list below provides examples (websites correct at time of printing).

Practice: Ateliers Jean Nouvel
Principal: Jean Nouvel
Website: www.jeannouvel.com

Practice: Santiago Calatrava
Principal: Santiago Calatrava
Website: www.calatrava.com

Practice: Foster & Partners
Principal: Lord Norman Foster
Website: www.fosterandpartners.com

Practice: Future Systems
Principals: Jan Kaplicky & Amanda Levete
Website: www.future-systems.com

Practice: Gehry Partners, LLP
Principal: Frank O. Gehry
Website: www.foga.com

Practice: Grimshaws (formerly Nicholas Grimshaw & Partners)
Principal: Sir Nicholas Grimshaw
Website: www.grimshaw-architects.com

Practice: Zaha Hadid Architects
Principal: Zaha Hadid
Website: www.zaha-hadid.com

Practice: Kendrick Bangs Kellogg, Global Architect
Principal: Kendrick Bangs Kellogg
Website: www.kendrickbangskellogg.com

BIBLIOGRAPHY & WEBSITES

Practice: OMA (Office for Metropolitan
  Architecture)
Principal: Rem Koolhaas
Website: www.oma.nl

Practice: John Lautner Associates
Principal: John Lautner (now deceased)
Website: www.johnlautner.org

Practice: Daniel Libeskind
Principal: Daniel Libeskind
Website: www.daniel-libeskind.com

Practice: EMBT
Principal: Enric Miralles (now deceased)
Wesbite: www.mirallestagliabue.com

Practice: Oscar Niemeyer
Principal: Oscar Niemeyer
Website: www.niemeyer.org

Practice: NIO Architecten
Principal: Maurice Nio
Website: www.nio.nl

Practice: Renzo Piano Building Workshop
Principal: Renzo Piano
Website: www.rpbw.com

Practice: Bart Prince - Architect
Principal: Bart Prince
Website: www.bartprince.com

Practice: Richard Rogers Partnership
Principal: Lord Richard Rogers
Website: www.richardrogers.co.uk

Practice: Kenzo Tange Associates
Principal: Kenzo Tange (now deceased)
Website: www.ktaweb.com

Practice: Tsui Design & Research Inc.
Principal: Dr. Eugene Tsui
Wesbite: www.tdrinc.com

Practice: Ugo Brunoni Architecte
Principal: Ugo Brunoni
Website: www.ugobrunoni.ch

The Sage, Gateshead, England — Foster & Partners created the arching canopy's three ridges.